£3.00

Dusty Wesker's Cookery Book

BY DUSTY WESKER

WITH ILLUSTRATIONS BY JO DELAFONS

Chatto & Windus LONDON

Published in 1987 by Chatto & Windus Ltd
30 Bedford Square, London WC1B 3RP

British Library Cataloguing in Publication Data

Wesker, Dusty
Dusty Wesker's cookery book.
1. Cookery, International
I. Title
641.5   TX725.AI

ISBN 0-7011-3131-4

Typeset at The Spartan Press Ltd, Lymington, Hants
Printed in Great Britain by Redwood Burn Ltd, Trowbridge, Wiltshire

Contents

Acknowledgements

I thank Gillian Freeman and Paula Jacobs who enthused about my cooking to Hilary Laurie. I'm grateful to Hilary Laurie and Chatto & Windus for having the faith to bring this book about. And I'm indebted to my husband who looked over my notes, goaded me on, surrendered to my stubbornness, typed the sheets, and whose diary I raided for details of events I'd forgotten.

To A.
husband, friend, support

Publisher's note and conversion tables

These recipes will feed 6–8 people, unless noted otherwise.

Both imperial and metric measurements are given. Use one or other set of measurements; do not mix the two.

It should be remembered that the American pint is 16 fl oz in comparison to the imperial pint, used in both Britain and Australia, which is 20 fl oz. The British standard tablespoon which has been used in this book holds 17.7 ml, the American 14.2 ml, and the Australian 20 ml. A teaspoon holds approximately 5 ml in all three countries.

Oven temperature chart

°C	°F	Gas mark	
110	225	¼	very slow
130	250	½	
140	275	1	slow
150	300	2	
170	325	3	
180	350	4	moderate
190	375	5	
200	400	6	moderately hot
220	425	7	hot
230	450	8	
240	475	9	very hot

Liquids

Imperial	Metric
2½ fl oz	75 ml
5 oz / ¼ pt	150 ml
10 oz / ½ pt	300 ml
20 oz / 1 pt	600 ml
1½ pt	900 ml
1¾ pt	1 litre
teaspoon	5 ml
dessertspoon	10 ml
tablespoon	15 ml

Solids

1 oz	25 g
2 oz	50 g
4 oz	100 g
8 oz	225 g
12 oz	325 g
14 oz	400 g
16 oz / 1 lb	450 g

Introduction

Some of my family and friends would describe me as a wicked cook. These are my sins:

I don't follow recipes all the way.

I don't weigh or measure quantities.

I worry if people don't ask for seconds.

I over-feed.

It may be that as a cook I have more cheek than talent. What is certain is that I have opportunity. Having a playwright for a husband means I cook everything from lunches for foreign directors, auditioning actors, thesis writers, journalists, constantly changing bank managers, to first-night parties and parties for entire visiting theatre companies. I've cooked for Nuria Espert's Spanish troupe, the Piccolo Theatre of Milan, the Habima of Tel Aviv. I've cooked for trade union leaders, politicians, Hollywood producers, foreign ambassadors, endless aunts, uncles, first, second and third cousins, and my own family. I *have* to cook.

Fortunately I love to cook. And in the process I've made discoveries and discovered an exuberant appetite for other people's appetites. This book, then, is for those who *have* to cook, enjoy cooking, are prepared to experiment, fail and try a second time. In these pages I hope to pass on not merely recipes I've discovered or invented, but a pleasure in feeding. And because friends around me have gone down like nine-pins with heart problems, I've tried to be conscious of 'healthy eating'. It's difficult! You'll find salads here and grilled foods, but I'm afraid I indulge.

It's a book for compulsive cook-book buyers, for bed-time reading. You will read not only explanations of why I chose what I chose to cook, and the problems encountered, but also a kind of journal of events leading up to the gatherings. I gossip about raspberry-picking excursions, stocking up foods in the cheap season, and about my family and friends. In fact I go here and there as anarchically as I sometimes cook.

After all, cooking is not an exact science. Not simply because individual tastes differ but because a cut of Scottish beef can require a slight variation in roasting from the same cut of French beef. There are different kinds of rice; different pastry is called for depending upon what you want to put inside; some apples have more juice than others. And so on. My recipes can only be guides for your intelligence, tastes, and your guests' appetites.

How did I begin? Early on in our marriage the playwright Bernard Kops and his wife, Erica, came for dinner and I burned the lamb chops. My husband bought me a huge tome called *The Gourmet Cookbook*. I don't remember how often I dipped into it, but it wasn't for long. Soon I took off on my own and found that the two biggest influences on me were the Jewish and English kitchens.

Many years ago I saw a marvellous play by N. F. Simpson called *The One-Way Pendulum* in which an old neighbour – played gloriously by Gwen Nelson – came into a house every Friday morning to eat the week's left-overs. My family and friends can always expect to find left-overs in *my* kitchen! Better to have left-overs than be the kind of person who invites friends to lunch and serves them a soused herring and half a hard-boiled egg. True! A friend swore it was what he'd been given. I can't bear mean natures.

This is not a book for mean natures. I was born poor and have never learned how to be careful. You'll have to apply the brakes yourself. This is a book for the impulsive, the generous, the care-free, and for those who spend so much time in the kitchen they desperately want their food eaten and relished.

Dusty Wesker
1987

Journal and Recipes

A. invited his new agent, Nathan Joseph, to lunch today with Claire Venables, artistic director of the Crucible Theatre in Sheffield. Claire is contemplating including a play or two of his in forthcoming seasons.

Dinner out tonight. Had to make lunch and rush off to the hairdresser's. Rarely join these working lunches anyway.

Decided on beef Stroganoff which I hadn't cooked for some time. Needs little preparation and is always tasty. Shopped for rump steak yesterday. Always like to be prepared well ahead. Discovered my local supermarket had chickens on special offer. Can't resist special offers. Idea came to make chopped liver as a starter. Bought three chickens on the spot. Will think about what to do with chickens later. They provided me with two very generous livers, and a lump of fat – schmaltz.

Nat said he was on a diet so bought baby avocados to offer him a salad as an alternative. Was also prepared to grill a steak for him, but when he arrived he announced that, as it was me who was feeding him, he'd decided to start his diet tomorrow!

Beef Stroganoff is usually served on a bed of fluffy rice, but for a change I piped creamed potatoes around the edge. Acts as garnish. For other vegetables I steamed mangetouts and spinach.

My mother had picked gooseberries for me last summer. I'd frozen them. Yesterday cooked them in preparation for today's dessert – gooseberry pie.

No meal is really complete without cheese and fresh fruit. But after three courses my guests had no more appetite.

Chopped Liver

1 large onion, chopped	Salt and pepper to taste
2 tablespoons chicken fat (scooped from inside chicken)	Livers from 3 chickens
	2 hard-boiled eggs, grated

Fry onion gently in chicken fat while it's melting. Add salt and pepper to taste. Remove onions when nicely brown. Leave aside.

Cook livers until well done. Mince. Stir in grated boiled egg, onions, chicken fat and all. Serve cold. Oddly, it always seems to taste better next day.

Beef Stroganoff

2 lb / 900 g rump steak	½ lb / 225 g button mushrooms
Freshly ground black pepper	10 fl oz / 300 ml sour cream
4 tablespoons butter	Salt to taste
2 tablespoons onion, finely chopped	Nutmeg

Cut steak across the grain into thin slices about 2 in / 5 cm long. Add black pepper. Put aside. Using half the butter, fry onions until light brown. Add meat to pan. Keep turning until all sides are brown. Do not overcook. Remove from pan but keep hot. Add remaining butter to pan and cook mushrooms. Stir in cream. Season to taste with salt and nutmeg. Remove pan from heat. Combine meat and onions with sauce. Serve immediately.

Gooseberry Pie

1½ lb / 700 g gooseberries	2 tablespoons water
3 oz / 75 g brown sugar	1 tablespoon cornflour

Cook gooseberries in water and brown sugar until soft but still whole. Remove with slotted spoon. Thicken juice with cornflour. Leave to cool.

Sweet pastry

7 oz / 200 g butter	1 tablespoon cold water
1 tablespoon icing sugar	12 oz / 350 g flour
1 egg	

Grease 8 in / 20 cm pie tin.

Whisk butter and icing sugar until light. Mix in egg and cold water. Fold in flour to form dough ball. Roll out as thin as possible and line pie tin. Place gooseberry mixture in shell. Cover with remaining pastry. Bake at 200°c / 400°F / gas mark 6 for 45 minutes.

New recipes often come into being because one hasn't got the exact ingredients! You're forced to improvise. Which is what happened this afternoon when I discovered what sounded like a lovely new cheesecake recipe and realised I had only half the cheese required. Eager pants! Had to try it there and then. Everything was wrong but turned out right. Added Greek yoghurt to make up the missing cheese. Put the mixture in the oven and remembered I'd forgotten to mix in the macaroons; crushed and sprinkled them on top instead. Turned out more moist than I expect was intended. Prefer my recipe!

As usual baked twice as much as I needed. To whom could I give it away? Called up my nephew-in-law, Adam, and my friend Mikki's son, Jonathan, two boys with healthy appetites – one not a boy, more a man of thirty about to be married. Delivered them each a generous portion of hot cake. Jonathan admired my prompt delivery. Said I was better than Interflora! Adam phoned later. Wished he'd not eaten his share at once. Wanted to taste it cooled down.

Sweet Cheese Tart

8 oz / 225 g shortcrust pastry	4 oz / 100 g full fat cream cheese
4 oz / 100 g macaroons, crushed	4 large eggs, separated
4 oz / 100 g walnuts, crushed	3 oz / 75 g castor sugar
5 fl oz / 150 ml double cream	3 oz / 75 g ground almonds
8 oz / 225 g Greek yoghurt	2 teaspoons nutmeg powder

Shortcrust pastry for flan case

6 oz / 175 g plain flour	1 egg yolk
3 oz / 75 g salted butter cut into cubes	1 tablespoon water

Rub butter into flour. Beat egg yolk with water. Make well in flour. Pour in beaten egg. Form dough with as little handling as possible. Leave to rest on floured surface in cool place for half an hour before using.

Grease 10 in / 25 cm flan tin. Line with pastry.

Mix macaroons and walnuts. Set aside. Whisk all other ingredients, except egg whites, in following order: cream, yoghurt, cheese, egg yolks, sugar, ground almonds, nutmeg. Whisk egg whites until stiff. Fold into creamed mixture. Pour into pastry shell.

Sprinkle macaroon and walnut mix on top. Bake at 190°C / 375°F / gas mark 5 for about 30 minutes until firm. Careful you do not overcook.

Friday
15 March

Just returned from four days in Copenhagen where we saw an English actress, Vivienne McKee, who runs a Danish-based theatre company, perform *Annie Wobbler*. She's had a huge success. Only a small 90-seat theatre but they're turning people away. Always a good feeling.

Arrived back at 7 p.m. Met at the airport by our youngest son, Daniel, and his girlfriend, Jo. Gratifying having one of your children meet you. By 8 p.m. actors began arriving for second round of auditions for *One More Ride On The Merry-Go-Round*. Went on all evening. Had to keep the coffee pot hot while actors bunched up around my kitchen table waiting nervously to give their nervous readings to playwright and director, Graeme Watkins, upstairs in the study. Meant I couldn't start to make the pastry for 300 mouth-sized quiches till much later.

Why 300 mouth-sized quiches? Sister-in-law, Della, is making a huge wedding for her son, Adam. The family has been marshalled to share some of the burden of cooking. I'd also volunteered to scrub 88 lb of potatoes to go with boiled salmon Della is preparing – among a dozen other dishes. I volunteered A. to make a box full of caramelised oranges.

Saturday
16 March

Last-minute shopping for such things as cream and eggs. Also had to collect my dress so it wasn't till around 1 p.m. that I was able to settle down to mix the concoctions for the quiches: asparagus, mushrooms fried with onions, and Gruyère cheese. All finely chopped and placed in separate basins. Then came the heavenly distraction – my new grand-daughter, who needed to be held, or rather I needed to hold her. She's lucky I don't eat her. When I managed to get back to the quiches another nephew, the older married one, Miles, delivered the 88 lb of new potatoes and the box of oranges. A.'s training as a pastry chef in the old Hungaria Restaurant comes in useful sometimes. But with his slow slicing and pottering around with boiled sugar, and my daughter Tanya's slow scrubbing of the spuds, and my heaving of the trays back and forth into the oven, and the fiddly filling of the tiny cups, come 5 p.m. I felt completely up the wall.

A. had earlier told me that his cousin Norma had complained she hadn't been given enough to do for the wedding. Phoned her for help. Within half an hour she and husband Mike were sitting round the kitchen table. Daniel joined in. A great time catching up with family news.

7 p.m.: sent A. to buy Chinese take-away, Tanya opened some bottles of wine, and we picnicked in our kitchen, seven of us. Chinese food spiced with gossip. But my poor husband. It was a long time since he'd been in a pastry kitchen. He was at it till midnight, slicing oranges and getting the caramelising all wrong.

Sunday 17 March

A. up early trying again to get the caramelising right. Accidentally gave him castor sugar. Two catastrophes later I belatedly suggested 'try granulated'. It worked, he got the right texture within twenty minutes. As everyone loved it I'll – grudgingly – let him include his recipe in my book.

Had to transport to the synagogue: four enormous pots filled with newly scrubbed potatoes covered with just enough water to ensure they didn't turn brown; three large dishes of caramelised oranges; two large baking pans piled high with 300 quiches, easy to slip in the oven and get warm for cocktails at five. No serious mishaps en route apart from a trail of caramel sauce across the car boot floor and over the rear bumper. Tacky!

Baby Quiches – for 50

2 lb / 900 g shortcrust pastry
24 eggs
3 pints / 1800 ml single cream

½ teaspoon nutmeg
1 teaspoon cayenne pepper
Salt to taste

See page 13 for shortcrust pastry. Cut out pastry with 3 in / 7 cm cutter. Press into petits-fours tins. Chosen ingredients: bacon, asparagus tips, onions, Gruyère cheese, courgettes, spinach or what you fancy, singly or in groups.

Blend eggs and cream. Add nutmeg, cayenne, salt. Fill pastry shells with ingredients. Pour mixture over them. Bake for 15 minutes at 190°C / 375°F / gas mark 5.

Caramelised Oranges – for 6

6 seedless oranges	2 tablespoons lemon juice
10 oz / 275 g granulated sugar	2 tablespoons orange liqueur
30 fl oz / 900 ml water	

Remove some of the rind from the oranges, taking care to leave the pith behind. Cut peel into matchstick-size pieces. Boil in 10 fl / 300 ml water to remove bitterness. Drain and set aside.

Boil sugar in 5 fl oz / 150 ml water. When tacky – test by putting spoon in boiling sugar syrup, then into cup of cold water – throw in pieces of peel. Boil for 8–10 minutes. Remove peel. Add ½ pint / 300 ml water to the pan of sugar syrup. When it begins to darken, add another 5 fl oz / 150 ml water. Be careful. Add the water very gently because it will splash. Bring to the boil, add lemon and liqueur. Pour over sliced oranges and scatter on the toffeed matchsticks of peel.

If you wish you can make a separate burnt sugar mixture and caramelise the peel. You can add more or less liqueur, or a different liqueur. I wonder what it would be like to add peppermint.

Friday
22 March Last night's dinner for eight included one of our oldest friends, Tom Maschler, A.'s publisher. Tom's a picker of bits and a sucker of bones. Usually rings the night before to say he's coming over to catch up on his and A.'s life. Always make him chopped liver but among the guests was Gillian Freeman, a writer friend from around the corner, who alerted me that her allergy was onions. Gave her migraine. No chopped liver! Worse, considering I cook practically everything with onions, I was confronted with an unprecedented challenge for the entire meal.

One of my most pleasurable culinary experiences was eating fresh scallops in Maine. Always held off cooking them in London, fearing they'd never be as fresh. Now, to replace chopped liver, I'd risk them as starters with fennel and spinach tossed in lots of garlic butter.

What else could work without onions? If the stuffing and seasoning were right, how about a leg of lamb? Wanted to avoid potatoes and decided that, if I assembled a variety of vegetables, that would further compensate for absence of onions. Mashed swedes, Jerusalem artichokes, parsnips flavoured with caraway seeds – couldn't be more varied than that!

To really help them forget they'd not been given their onions, decided to spoil them with two desserts: a Grand Marnier cream with sliced strawberries and left-over strips of caramelised orange peel, and a blackcurrant crumble.

The onion problem confronted me again when it came to making the gravy. Who's ever heard of gravy without onions? God knows why, but decided to add white wine to the water in which I'd boiled the lamb bones. And of course plenty of seasoning and thickening.

For stuffing lots of fresh rosemary (which is the one herb that really thrives in my garden), dried apricots, pine nuts, breadcrumbs, all bound together with a cup of dry vermouth. Went over the top and concocted a marinade of mustard, soya sauce and honey to pour over the lamb. Stuffed and marinated the night before, so that the meat would be saturated with the flavours. Attacked from inside and out as it were.

My aim in making two desserts was to provide choice. Six asked for helpings of both on one plate. Two thought one would suffice but seemed unable to resist sampling the second. Cleaned plates. Lots of sighs. Very gratifying. I love food-sighs. Our youngest son's girl-friend sits at the kitchen table and no matter what I cook for her she sighs ' . . . mmm . . . mmm . . .' with each mouthful. Pleases me.

On reflection, I think the scallops would have made a better hors d'oeuvre had they been larger than the ones I'd bought. Remained terrified of giving my guests upset stomachs. Knew they were fresh but, in my anxiety, left them over-long in water. Too much moisture was absorbed. But the pleasure of new recipes is that one can look forward to improving them next time, and my mistakes are your gain.

Added to the challenge of puzzling out a menu with no onions was the distraction of a kitchen full of actors waiting to audition for *One More Ride On The Merry-Go-Round*, a bawdy comedy, begun in

1978, which no one dared present till now. Opens at the Phoenix, Leicester, on 25 April. Began at 10 a.m. and kept going through to 5 p.m. Doorbell constantly ringing, coffee pot needing to be kept topped up. Of course it was the bustling cook who attracted the actors' nervous conversation. But who's the biggest show-stopper of all? Every actor knows: Babies. My five-week-old grand-daughter, Natasha, was also visiting and everything tends to grind to a halt when she's around. So glad I marinated lamb the day before. Guests arrived at 8 p.m. by which time fire was lit.

Scallops with Spinach and Fennel

1½ lb / 650 g small scallops
8 oz / 225 g frozen leaf spinach
2 tablespoons butter
2 cloves crushed garlic

1 large head of fennel, finely sliced
Salt and pepper to taste

Wash and drain scallops thoroughly. Thaw spinach well and drain every last drop of water. Toss scallops in a tablespoon of butter with garlic for 5 minutes. Remove from pan but keep hot. Cook fennel in remainder of butter for 5 minutes. Add spinach. When warmed through remove from heat and combine with scallops. Season to taste.

Stuffed Leg of Lamb

4½ lb / 2 kg leg of lamb with bone removed

Stuffing

2 tablespoons fresh rosemary, chopped
6 oz / 175 g breadcrumbs
½ lb / 225 g boiled dried apricots

¼ lb / 225 g pine nuts
5 fl oz / 150 ml dry vermouth
Salt and pepper to taste

Marinade

3 dessertspoons of honey
1 dessertspoon of French mustard

2 tablespoons soya sauce

Mix ingredients for the stuffing and press it into cavity left by bone.

Tie meat up with string to secure contents. Pour marinade over it. Leave in fridge for the night. Cook for two hours at 190°C / 375°F / gas mark 5.

Parsnips

3 large parsnips, peeled and   1 tablespoon butter
   sliced   1 teaspoon caraway seeds

Boil parsnips for five minutes in salted water. Drain. Put into ovenproof dish. Dot with butter and caraway seeds. Bake at 190°C / 375°F / gas mark 5 for 30 minutes.

Mashed Swede

1 large swede, cut in small pieces   1 dessertspoon of butter

Boil pieces of swede in salted water. Drain and mash with butter.

Jerusalem Artichokes

1 lb / 450 g artichokes   2 tablespoons breadcrumbs
1 medium onion (optional)   1 oz / 25 g butter
½ pt / 300 ml chicken stock   Salt and pepper to taste
2 tablespoons single cream

Wash and peel artichokes. Parboil them in salted water for ten minutes. When cold, drain and cut into thin slices. Similarly, parboil the onion and cut into rings. Place in ovenproof dish with chicken stock and cream. Season. Sprinkle breadcrumbs on top. Dot with butter. Bake at 180°C / 350°F / gas mark 4 until pale brown.

Blackcurrant Crumble

1½ lb / 650 g blackcurrants   8 oz / 225 g sugar

Cook blackcurrants and sugar in half a cup of water for about 5 minutes. Place in ovenproof dish.

Crumble mix

1 lb / 450 g fresh breadcrumbs   ½ lb / 225 g castor sugar
½ lb / 225 g ground almonds   ½ lb / 225 g butter

Rub breadcrumbs, ground almonds and castor sugar evenly into butter. Sprinkle on top of blackcurrants. Bake for 30 minutes at 200°c / 400°f / gas mark 6.

Grand Marnier Custard

12 fl oz / 350 ml single cream	4 eggs
3 tablespoons Grand Marnier	¼ lb / 100 g sugar

Gently boil up cream with Grand Marnier. Set aside. Beat eggs and sugar till light. Add hot cream stirring constantly. Pour into an ovenproof dish. Set in pan of water. Bake for 45 minutes at 170°c / 325°f / gas mark 3.

The sweet custard is a good partner for the tarty crumble.

Tuesday 26 March

Yesterday Nichola McAuliffe came to be photographed for *Spotlight* by Daniel, my youngest. As usual, made more than enough supper, so suggested she stayed. A. wrote *Annie Wobbler* specially for Nichola. She's become a family friend, which rarely happens with actors. Some weeks ago she and I plotted one of my future dinner parties with old Wesker actors she'd wanted to meet. It was to be a 'shop talk' dinner with lots of laughs.

Sometimes I try to guess what my guests would like to eat. We agreed they'd go for fillet of beef rolled in puff pastry. As we discussed the menu during supper, I realised with horror I'd forgotten our bank manager was coming for lunch next day and I'd done no shopping! Fortunately had ingredients for a cheesecake and, as it's always best made the day before, I could at least start on that.

When I'd invited Jim O'Halloran, the new bank manager (he's the assistant bank manager actually but he's the one who deals with our level of income!), he'd asked if he could bring along a colleague, Chris Powell, who'd had to study A.'s plays at school in Bristol. How could I say no?

No time to try and guess what they'd like, so opted for trout which *I* love. Normally enjoy it grilled but found what seemed like a good recipe – stuffed with fennel, haddock and onions. Turned out to be trout with a delicious flavour.

Made two starters because one was avocado with prawns and I always imagine there'll be at least one person with an aversion to shellfish. The other was my old faithful chopped liver.

With the creamy cheesecake served succulent Spanish strawberries which are now available.

The assistant bank manager immediately assumed first-name terms. 'Dusty' had the pleasure of feeding 'Jim and Chris' who turned out to be eager young men with good appetites who enjoyed their food. They felt so at home they decided it had been a mistake not to have invited the bank manager as well! Perhaps it was the bottle of Chablis. Not a *premier cru*, but a good '83 brought to us by a petite Japanese professor who turned up unexpectedly on our doorstep last Sunday . . . but that's another story.

Avocado Prawn Cocktail – for 4

8 oz / 225 g prawns	1 crushed clove garlic
1 dessertspoon lemon juice	Salt and pepper to taste
1 tablespoon mayonnaise	2 large avocados

Combine prawns with lemon juice, mayonnaise and garlic. Salt and pepper to taste. Fill cavity of avocados with cocktail.

Stuffed Trout – for 4

8 oz / 225 g skinned haddock	4 whole trout, boned
1 egg white	1 large red pepper
5 fl oz / 150 ml single cream	2 oz / 50 g butter
4 oz / 100 g chopped fennel	1 fish stock cube
2 oz / 50 g chopped onion	5 fl oz / 150 ml hot water
Salt and pepper to taste	

Put haddock, egg white, cream, fennel and onion in liquidiser and make a cream, adding salt and pepper to taste. With this, stuff trout. Lay in a flat pan. Slice red pepper into strips and lay around the fish. Dot with butter. Melt fish stock cube in hot water and cover trout with stock. Wrap pan in tin foil and bake for 30 minutes at 180°C / 350°F / gas mark 4.

Cheesecake

8 oz / 225 g digestive biscuits	1½ lb / 650 g curd cheese
1 oz / 25 g butter	Vanilla essence or lemon to taste
5 eggs	15 fl oz / 400 ml sour cream
6 oz / 175 g castor sugar	

Crush biscuits and mix with melted butter. Press into loose-bottomed 8 in / 20 cm cake tin. Separate eggs. Whip egg whites first to stiff peaks. Whisk yolks, sugar, cheese and vanilla or lemon for 10 minutes. Fold in egg whites. Pour into cake tin. Bake for 35 minutes at 180°C / 350°F / gas mark 4. Remove from oven, leave to cool slightly, then pour whipped sour cream over top and replace in oven for further 10 minutes. The unusual feature of this recipe is that you now withdraw the cake from the oven and immediately place in fridge to cool.

This cake can be served with fresh fruit in season, sliced and decorating the top.

Monday
1 April

It's been a hard day's weekend!

Cast party on Saturday night. Newspaper men and wives on Sunday night. It was not only the cast and technicians of *One More Ride On The Merry-Go-Round* for whom I was cooking, but 'others'. There are always 'others'. People who come from abroad. Friends A. wants to see. 'Let them all come,' he says. And why not? Claude Mayer, the French-Canadian director who'd directed *Chips With Everything* in Montreal, was in town studying with the BBC on a TV director's course; and Neville Shulman, accountant and personal manager of Twiggy, among others. A. wanted to interest him in the British Centre of the ITI (International Theatre Institute); and there was his wife, Emma.

Started cooking on Friday. One of my favourite chocolate cakes with raisins soaked overnight in rum. Then the trifle, always needs to be done the day before, especially as I make it with more ingredients than the average recipe calls for. (You'll find my recipe on page 58.) Eating through it is to discover and experience many different tastes and textures.

My dear friend, William Frankel, ex-editor of the *Jewish Chronicle*, adores gefillte fish. Had to make that. Lasagne is good for large gatherings and survives overnight in a fridge. That next. Was also able to prepare masses of chopped vegetables ready for a stir fry. Had to stop because we were due at the Royal Court to see *Tom And Viv*. Realised I'd been on my feet all day cooking and coping with endless telephone calls.

The most distressing call was for A. concerning his TV adaptation of Arthur Koestler's *Thieves In The Night*. The Israeli partner, Zvi

Spielman, rang to announce that the bloody French director was re-writing his scripts! A cavalier act not sanctioned by the German TV company, NDR, who were the main, the only, sponsors. Zvi had also been involved with a new film just premiered, *Not Quite Jerusalem*, which had been made from an excellent play by Paul Kember. The critics had panned it. A. wasn't aware of this when he spoke sternly to Zvi over the phone about the shabby betrayal of his Koestler script. Zvi was supposed to join us at the theatre but now considered it unwise! Problems! Problems! When not?

Began Saturday morning to roll out puff pastry for the chicken pies. Hadn't cheated this time; I'd made it earlier in the week. Meanwhile boiled the chickens and took the meat off the bones. The liquid from the five chickens was so concentrated that it turned into a delicious jelly clogged with all the vegetables I'd put into the chicken pot. Threw the lot into my chicken pies together with heaps of button mushrooms.

Potatoes next. Not that we need them, but some people like potatoes with whatever they eat. Baked potatoes with cheese; coleslaw and green salad. And, finally, a selection of sweets which I hopefully gauged would also feed my Sunday night dinner guests!

Fed twenty-five on Saturday night. Over-catered as usual. Not my fault this time; I'd let it be known the actors could bring partners. The message didn't reach them. Except one. Nor did any of the technicians turn up. The administrator, set designer, two publicity girls (and a boy-friend) were the non-acting representatives. Not that left-overs worry me; my kids invite their friends and have a good time. But why are people so casual about agreed arrangements? Drives me mad.

Successful party nevertheless. We always feel cast get-togethers break the ice for what's a hair-raising swim to the first night. Think the actors appreciated it. I'll know by how many write to say thank-you. Enjoy feeding them because it gives me a degree of involvement in A.'s plays, the activity around which is mostly remote for me. Though no one will ever know what it's like being the wife of a playwright, listening to the nightly reports, the rise and fall of fears and exhilarations, the dreaded approach of first nights, and the aftermath

of reviews which I have to read first in order that A. can by-pass the cruel and stupid ones.

Sunday was a relatively easy day because I'd already prepared the carp and the fish balls. My main course was pheasant which I cooked in red wine with braised fennel, and fried, flat mushrooms. Thank God some lemon cake was left over from the cast party, but to be safe I offered an alternative of sliced peaches and kiwi.

Sunday's guest of honour was Herbert Pundig, the editor of the Danish newspaper *Politiken*, and his wife, Susie. He brought as a gift a copy of a new book called *Israel's Lebanon War*. The Pundigs live half the time in Israel and the rest in Copenhagen. A vivid man, restless. Must be brilliant to edit a newspaper from afar. He feels the Lebanon war was a disastrous blunder. *Israel's Lebanon War*, by two Israeli journalists, which Herbert wanted A. to read, exposed the culprits in the Israeli hierarchy who'd led Israel into the war. 'Depressing and uplifting,' he declared it.

To meet him, I'd invited William Shawcross whom we got to know through A.'s brief encounter with the *Sunday Times*, and his wife, Michel, and William and Clare Frankel. Clare's one of the best cooks I know. Do I work harder when she's invited? Pointless if so, because Clare rang to say William was down with flu. That meant six at the dinner table. When it was over we decided six was probably the best number to have. Conversation is concentrated rather than fragmented. Nor is William the only one to adore stuffed carp. Me too!

Lasagne

Lasagne is a three-part operation: you need to make 2 different sauces and prepare the pasta. But it is a flexible dish; you can increase the quantity if you wish to.

Grease a 12 in / 30 cm ovenproof dish, 3 in / 7 cm deep.

Meat sauce

1 large onion, chopped
2 streaky rashers bacon, chopped
2 tablespoons vegetable oil
8 oz / 225 g chicken livers

1 lb / 450 g lean minced beef
1 clove garlic, crushed
3 tablespoons tomato purée
Salt and pepper to taste

Using a saucepan, fry chopped onions and bacon in vegetable oil for 10 minutes. Add chopped livers and minced beef. Cook for 5 minutes, then add garlic, tomato purée, salt and pepper. Simmer for 1 hour with lid on.

Cheese sauce

2 oz / 50 g butter	4 oz / 100 g Gruyère cheese,
2 oz / 50 g flour	grated
1 pint / 600 ml milk	2 oz / 50 g Parmesan cheese,
½ teaspoon powdered bay leaf	grated
2 teaspoons nutmeg	Salt and pepper to taste

Using a saucepan, melt butter and blend flour to make a roux. Gradually let out with milk till a creamy sauce. Add bayleaf, nutmeg, both cheeses, salt and pepper. Leave aside.

Pasta

Try to buy fresh pasta. If unavailable, dried pasta will do, though it's second best.

8 oz / 225 g pasta, wide and flat	1 teaspoon salt
3 pints / 1.8 litres water	1 dessertspoon vegetable oil

Using a saucepan, bring water, oil and salt to boil. Put in pasta. Boil for 15 minutes with lid on. Drain. Rinse with cold water to help separate them. Lay strips of pasta on teatowel to avoid them sticking together.

Assembly: Pour half of meat sauce over base of dish. Lay half the number of pasta strips over it. Pour half of cheese sauce over pasta strips. Pour remaining meat sauce over cheese sauce. Add remaining strips of pasta. Pour last of cheese sauce on top. Bake at 180°C / 350°F / gas mark 4 for one hour.

Chicken Pie

I buy chickens when I find them on special offer. Although initial outlay is large, in the end it's cheaper to buy four at a time. It's also useful to have a supply of chicken meat which can be used for a variety of dishes: stuffed crêpes, pilaus, curries, pies. I boil them, two at a time, in 3 pints / 1.8 litres of water with two large onions, ½ lb / 225 g of carrots and 4 sticks of celery, salt and pepper to taste. I cook them for an hour and then use the same juice for cooking the second batch. This gives me a concentrated stock. I remove all flesh from bones, discard the skin, but retain the stock with vegetables.

1 lb / 450 g boiled chicken	5 fl oz / 150 ml milk
2 oz / 50 g butter	Salt and pepper to taste
2 oz / 50 g flour	6 oz / 175 g puff pastry
5 fl oz / 150 ml chicken stock	1 beaten egg for glazing

Put chicken meat into ovenproof pie dish. Extract desired quantity of vegetables from stock. Place with chicken meat.

Melt butter, add flour to make roux. Let out gradually with stock and milk to make smooth sauce. Season to taste. Pour over chicken. Lay puff pastry on top. Glaze with beaten egg. Bake at 220°C / 425°F / gas mark 7, for 30 minutes.

Baked Potatoes with Cheese

3 oz / 75 g Gruyère cheese, grated	Salt and pepper to taste
2 tablespoons Parmesan cheese, grated	1 oz / 25 g butter
	4 large potatoes, thinly sliced
½ teaspoon nutmeg	2 eggs, beaten
1 clove garlic	5 fl oz / 150 ml double cream

Mix seasonings with Gruyère and Parmesan cheese. Grease a shallow dish with the butter. Place layers of potatoes in the dish spreading some of seasoning and cheese between each layer. Combine eggs and cream and pour over potatoes. Sprinkle remaining seasoning and cheese over the top. Cover with tin foil. Bake at 190°C / 375°F / gas mark 5 for 40 minutes. Remove tin foil and bake for another 10 minutes to brown top.

Stuffed Carp

4 lb / 1.8 kg carp	1 tablespoon cold water
2 fish stock cubes	1 tablespoon ground almonds
1 pint / 600 ml water	3 tablespoons medium matzo
2 lb / 900 g minced fish	meal
3 medium onions, grated	8 oz / 225 g carrots, sliced
1 tablespoon vegetable oil	Sugar, salt and pepper to taste

The minced fish is usually cod, bream, whiting or haddock, available ready-minced from most fishmongers.

Dissolve fish stock cubes in 1 pint / 600 ml of water. In a bowl mix minced fish, grated onions, oil, water, ground almonds, matzo meal, castor sugar, salt and pepper. Fill the carp with mixture. Place in fish kettle surrounded by fish stock and sliced carrots. Steam for 1½ hours. Serve cold.

If you have no fish kettle, wrap stuffed fish in tin foil and bake in a moderate oven for 1½ hours. Omit fish stock, because baked fish makes its own juice.

Pheasant in Red Wine

1 pheasant	1 medium onion, sliced
1 bay leaf	2 sticks celery, finely chopped
1 sprig parsley	2 cooking apples, cored and
10 fl oz / 300 ml water	chopped
2 tablespoons plain flour	10 fl oz / 300 ml red wine
1 tablespoon vegetable oil	Salt and pepper to taste

Remove giblets from gutted pheasant. Joint bird leaving carcass whole. Using large deep frying pan, simmer carcass and giblets in water with bay leaf, parsley and seasonings for 30 minutes. Strain and reserve stock. Coat pheasant joints in flour. Fry on all sides in oil. Lower heat under pan and add onions, celery and apples. Cook until soft, approx. 10 minutes. Add wine and stock. Put in ovenproof dish, cover and bake for 1 hour at 170°C / 325°F / gas mark 3.

Chocolate Rum Raisin Cake

6 oz / 175 g raisins	8 oz / 225 g soft brown sugar
10 fl oz / 300 ml rum	4 oz / 100 g butter
8 oz / 225 g plain flour	2 eggs
½ teaspoon baking powder	
4 tablespoons drinking chocolate	

Put raisins into rum, cover and soak for 2 hours. Grease 8 in / 2.5 cm tin. Mix flour, baking powder, drinking chocolate and sugar. Rub butter into mixture. Make a well in mixture. Beat eggs and pour into well. Slowly mix. Add rum and raisins. Bake for 1½ hours at 150°C / 300°F / gas mark 2.

Lemon Cake

6 eggs, separated
6 oz / 175 g castor sugar
Grated rind and juice of
    2 lemons

4 oz / 100 g plain flour
10 fl oz / 300 ml double
    cream

Grease three 8 in / 20 cm sponge tins.

Whip egg whites. Beat yolks, sugar, lemon rind and juice until creamy. Fold in flour. Fold in egg whites. Pour and divide mixture between the 3 tins. Bake 170°C / 325°F / gas mark 3 for 45 minutes. Cool on rack. Whip cream, and spread between sponge layers and on top. You can flavour cream with lemon if you wish, and decorate the cake with toasted almonds.

Monday
15 April
Entertaining can be hair-raising! A weekend of cooking, let-downs and uncertainties.

A. has been in Leicester following rehearsals of *One More Ride On The Merry-Go-Round*, re-writing, as he does constantly, even plays long ago performed and in print. Came back on Saturday afternoon to find me in a panic over the Sunday lunch I was making for 23 members of the visiting Japanese company of Suzuki. We'd seen them in their festival theatre in Togamura two years ago. I loved their production of *The Trojan Women* which they'd continued playing in the open through a heavy rain storm. A. was not quite as enamoured. The director had given a party for all the visiting companies. I wanted to return hospitality during their four-day stay at the Riverside Studios, present them a good Sunday lunch, show them the inside of an English home.

They were having such success, turning people away, that they'd agreed to do an extra Sunday matinée performance, after my lunch!

The news came to me by accident. Rang A. in Leicester to cry help. He was at an evening rehearsal. Couldn't reach him. Rang David Gothard, the outgoing director of Riverside, asked when it had been decided to have the matinée. They had decided on Thursday! Why hadn't anybody thought to ring me? He apologised. Should I call it off? I asked. No, he begged. They'd be so disappointed. Agreed to go ahead but now came another problem. Don't actors prefer not to eat before a performance? How much should I cook? Perhaps if I didn't over-provide, I'd end up providing just enough!

Sunday morning brought new rumblings. I'd invited some British theatre people to share hosting the Japanese with me. Howard Brenton rang to ask if it was today he was invited to lunch and if so, could I give him our address again because he'd misplaced it! What's happening to us all? One tries hard to make things work for others but the supports are constantly being pulled away.

My guests for Saturday night were to be our old friends Gordon and Cressida Wasserman whom we'd not seen for a long time. Gordon is Canadian and works for the Ministry of Environment. Cressida is a daughter of Hugh and Dora Gaitskell. Also Guy Slater and his girl-friend, Julia Scofield. A. met Guy when he was in Cuba. His father was the British Ambassador, and Guy was there on holiday with his then wife, the actress, Helen Ryan. Guy was celebrating having resigned from being a BBC TV producer. He was going back to writing and freelance directing. The last couple invited were David Edgar and his wife, Eve Brook. A. became close to and fond of David through their work on the International Playwrights Committee.

Saturday morning Gordon rang to ask if he could bring his mother along. She was visiting from Canada. Of course he could. Not only had she entertained us when we were in Montreal, but I'm constantly doing that to my friends. People arrive all the time from abroad and we can't leave them at home when we're invited out for a delicious meal.

Guy and Julia arrived first, the Wassermans followed. By eight-thirty I had an intuition about the Edgars and rang them in their home in Birmingham. They were there! David was mortified. They'd just returned from Florence. Eve had told me they'd stay in London on their return, come to dinner and go on to Birmingham next day. Said she would have to check with David but was sure it would be all right. Each had then imagined the other had told me they wouldn't make it. A letter arrived today (as I guessed it would) full of explanations and apologies, ending 'Will you ever forgive us?' Replied: 'Of course I'll forgive you – one day!'

Nothing, however, could spoil the occasion. Five out of my seven Saturday guests asked for seconds of the starter. A new recipe, smoked salmon and spinach in puff pastry, which I'd discovered in Denmark. Easy to make. Can be prepared the day before and popped in the oven half an hour before guests arrive. This time I cheated and bought made-up puff pastry. It's fine.

To follow, I cooked duck on a rack with lots of black pepper. Duck needs orange sauce but, to give it an extra kick, I fried onions and puréed them together with the sauce. Baked mashed swede and parsnip covered with honey along with the duck. And broad beans. The meal desperately needed a salad before going on to raspberry flan – made from the last of my frozen raspberries. Sad. But this year is passing so quickly that July can't be far away, and I'll be able to go fruit-picking again.

Smoked Salmon and Spinach Tart

1 lb / 450 g puff pastry
2 lb / 900 g frozen spinach
  leaves

12 oz / 350 g smoked salmon
5 fl oz / 150 ml of single cream
2 eggs

Line swiss roll tin with half of the puff pastry, rolled thin. Thaw spinach well and drain every last drop of water. Put layer of salmon on to pastry, followed by a layer of spinach, followed by the remaining salmon. Beat eggs and cream, adding black pepper to taste. Pour over filling. Cover the filling with second half of pastry. Bake at 200°C / 400°F / gas mark 6 in top part of oven for 20 minutes.

Roast Duck with Spiced Orange Sauce

1 duck or duck joints
5 fl oz / 150 ml white wine

Salt and pepper to taste

Season duck with salt and pepper. Pierce skin to drain fat. (Keep fat for roasting potatoes.) Roast at 200°C / 400°F / gas mark 6, allowing 30 minutes to the pound. After one hour drain off fat. Continue roasting and basting with white wine until cooked. Retain juice which has now collected in bottom of pan to mix with orange sauce. Joint the duck and pour the sauce over.

Orange sauce

3 oranges	Juice of one lemon
6 oz / 175 g sugar	2 sticks of cinnamon
2 tablespoons water	1 dessertspoon of arrowroot

Cut unpeeled oranges into ¼ in / 6 mm slices. Boil water, sugar, lemon juice and cinnamon sticks to form a syrup. Add orange slices. Simmer until rind is soft. Thicken with arrowroot.

Raspberry Flan

Line 10 in / 25 cm flan tin with almond pastry (see page 109). Bake blind for 30 minutes at 190°C / 375°F / gas mark 5. Leave to cool.

Crème pâtissière

2 egg yolks	1 dessertspoon brandy
2 oz / 50 g sugar	1½ lb / 700 g raspberries
½ oz / 14 g cornflour	8 oz / 225 g jar redcurrant jelly
5 fl oz / 400 ml milk	

Separate egg. Blend 2 yolks with sugar and flours. Add sufficient milk to make a paste. Heat remainder of milk. When hot add to the paste and return to the saucepan to thicken. Leave to cool. When cool, add brandy and spread mixture on pastry base. Cover with raspberries. Glaze with slightly heated redcurrant jelly.

The English guests invited to meet the Japanese for Sunday lunch were Howard Brenton and his wife and their delightfully bright son; Frank and Mary Barrie – Frank very relieved to have finished five months of *The Way Of The World* at the Haymarket. They were off on holiday and so wouldn't be at the first night of *One More Ride* in which their daughter was playing a part. Nichola came, full of helpful buzzing around, serving, filling glasses. And Howard Davies, who has directed in Japan.

At about 1 p.m. a fleet of taxis arrived. In trooped 23 actors and technicians. We stood at the door saying: 'Welcome, welcome, welcome.' Twenty-three times! They took off their coats, piled their bags and sacks under the hall table, entered the lounge and sat around on what seats there were. The unlucky ones took to the floor. They seemed at home there.

I asked A. to give a welcome speech and explain how we'd originally planned to give them a relaxed afternoon. We knew they had to rush back to a performance, but they must not worry and should only eat and drink what they felt able to. We needn't have apologised. They ate and drank everything. So much that it sent me scurrying into the kitchen to boil up a few potatoes and vegetables to provide my family with something to eat!

I'd cooked monkfish with prawns mixed in rice; a pot of fresh noodles, imagining these would suit the Japanese, who might be less adventurous in their eating habits. In addition I made sweet and sour meatballs in mushroom sauce. A roast turkey is always a safe thing, stuffed with a simple sage and onion stuffing; new potatoes roasted in lovely duck-fat, left over from the night before. Filled one bowl with chopped celery and spring onions, another with plain green salad.

And of course desserts, the dishes I most enjoy cooking, and without which no party of mine is ever complete. Pecan pie, caramelised oranges and Pavlovas filled with lychees and apricots. Used the egg whites left over from making the crème patissière for my raspberry tart the night before. Who said the Japanese don't like desserts! Everything got eaten. Two hours later the fleet of taxis came to take them, heavy-laden, away. Wonder what their performance was like.

About ten of us remained sitting amid the débris. But as I have helpful children, the cleaning-up was soon done. Howard Brenton was in the middle of rehearsals for *Pravda*, the play he'd written with David Hare on journalism. Howard confessed he and David had read A.'s book on journalism but not his play, *The Journalists*, for fear they'd be influenced! Howard said he'd arrange first night tickets for us. We're happy their play on journalism is being done; bewildered as to why ours isn't.

Monkfish and Prawns in Rice

Large tail of monkfish, skinned,
about 2 lb / 1 kg
5 fl oz / 150 ml white wine
10 fl oz / 300 ml water
1 medium onion
Grated rind of 1 lemon

Salt and pepper to taste
1 lb / 450 g prawns
2 oz / 50 g butter
2 cloves garlic, crushed
1 lb / 450 g Basmati rice

Poach monkfish with wine, water, onion, lemon rind, salt and pepper for 20 minutes. Take fish off bone and flake. Keep warm. Retain stock.

Toss prawns in butter and garlic, salt and pepper, for 5 minutes. Keep warm.

Cook rice in fish stock. Mix in monkfish and prawns. Garnish with watercress.

Meatballs in Sweet and Sour Mushroom Sauce

1 lb / 450 g minced veal
1 lb / 450 g minced pork
3 eggs
6 oz / 175 g breadcrumbs
1 tablespoon freshly chopped
parsley

1 medium onion, chopped
2 tablespoons vegetable oil
Salt and pepper to taste

Mix together veal, pork, eggs, breadcrumbs, parsley, salt and pepper. Roll into balls the size of an egg. Cook onions in vegetable oil. Add meat balls, brown them on all sides. Put aside in casserole.

Sweet & sour sauce

4 oz / 100 g mushrooms
1 beef stock cube
10 fl oz / 300 ml water
1 oz / 25 g butter

½ tablespoon flour
2 teaspoons sugar
1 tablespoon lemon juice
Salt and pepper to taste

Wash and slice mushrooms. Simmer in beef stock for 30 minutes. Melt butter in separate saucepan. Add flour to make roux. Gradually let out with half the stock until a creamy consistency. Blend in remaining stock along with mushrooms. Add sugar, lemon juice, salt and pepper to taste. Bring to boil and cook for 5 minutes. Pour sauce over meatballs. Cover and bake at 190°C / 375°F / gas mark 5 for 30 minutes.

Roast Turkey with Sage and Onion Stuffing

16 lb / 7 kg turkey   Salt and pepper to taste
2 oz / 50 g butter

Stuffing

1 chicken stock cube   1 medium onion, chopped
10 fl oz / 300 ml hot water   1 dessertspoon dried sage
½ lb / 225 g breadcrumbs   1 oz / 25 g butter

Dissolve chicken stock in hot water with 1 oz / 25 g butter. Mix in breadcrumbs, sage and onion. Salt and pepper to taste. Fill turkey with stuffing. Spread 2 oz / 50 g butter over breast. Salt and pepper to taste. Wrap loosely in tin foil. Place in baking tin. Roast for 4 hours at 200°C / 400°F / gas mark 6. Take off foil. Turn turkey on to its knees. Roast for another hour. This allows breast to soak up and become saturated with juices in pan.

Pecan Pie in Shortcrust Pastry

½ lb / 225 g shortcrust pastry   2 oz / 50 g butter, melted
3 eggs   8 oz / 225 g golden syrup or
4 oz / 100 g dark brown sugar   dark corn syrup
1 teaspoon vanilla   8 oz / 225 g pecan nuts
¼ teaspoon salt

Line 8 in / 20 cm tin with pastry (see page 13).

Whisk eggs, sugar, vanilla and salt. While whisking, gradually add melted butter. Add syrup and nuts. Or lay nuts on the pastry first, and then cover with mixture. Bake at 190°C / 375°F / gas mark 5 for 40 minutes.

Pavlova with Lychees and Apricots

1 pint / 600 ml double cream   Large tin of lychees
½ teaspoon vanilla   ½ lb / 225 g fresh apricots,
1 oz / 25 g castor sugar   sliced

8 oz / 225 g castor sugar	Pinch of salt
2 teaspoons cornflour	2 teaspoons vinegar
4 egg whites	1 teaspoon vanilla

Grease 2 swiss roll tins. Line tins with greased paper.

Mix cornflour and sugar.

Whisk egg whites and pinch of salt until stiff. Gradually add sugar and cornflour mixture. Next add vinegar and teaspoon vanilla.

Pipe meringue mixture on to paper in two circular shapes about 9 in / 22 cm diameter. Bake at 150°C / 300°F / gas mark 2 for 45 minutes, until crisp to touch. Remove from tins. Turn meringues over. *Very* carefully peel off paper. Return to oven for further 10 minutes – to dry out the backside (if you'll forgive the expression!). Remove from oven and allow to cool.

Whip 1 pint / 600 ml of double cream with ½ teaspoon of vanilla and 1 oz / 25 g of castor sugar. Spread cream on cooled meringue base. Pile with lychees and sliced apricots. Cover with second meringue.

You can make your filling with any number of mixed or individual fresh or tinned fruits. The cream can be lemon or coffee flavoured, or enriched by a liqueur. Your fruit can soak overnight in rum, brandy, port, what you fancy. You can even have an 'every & anything Pavlova'.

With time and energy one tries to make dinner parties memorable. Not sure what my guests will remember of last Saturday's dinner but I'll remember the horrendous price I had to pay for fillet steak. Reader beware! This one, which I plotted together with Nichola McAuliffe, is for special occasions.

Monday 22 April

'Which of his other actors do you want to meet?' I asked her. 'Frank Finlay?' she dared. Done. He'd played A.'s father in *Chicken Soup With Barley* and made his name as Corporal Hill in *Chips With Everything*. 'Ian McKellen?' she dared again. Yes. Always liked Ian. He'd played the lead in *Their Very Own And Golden City*. Ian had come to the last performance of *Annie Wobbler* and bounced into Nichola's dressing room with lots of praise. She'd been bowled over. His friend, Sean Mathias, a young playwright, had told her he'd like to meet A. if only to find out how he coped with bad reviews! Like a caged tiger! No one better to talk to! A. asked could he add someone to the list. Janet Suzman. Someone he'd always admired. Not a Wesker actor but he hoped she would be one day. Think he wanted to interest her in a revival of *The Four Seasons*. He'd been paring and rewriting.

Invitations had gone out at once. I'd given a lot of notice so could afford to wait. Time passed. No replies. I could end up with a meal but no guests! Chased Ian and finally got confirmation. Chased Frank who asked me to wait as he didn't know if he and Doreen would want to be in their Welsh cottage that weekend. It always surprises me when people don't make the imaginative leap into other people's situations. Couldn't he understand I had to know in time to be able to invite someone else? They finally declined. Nichola was in the kitchen at the time I made the last desperate call. Without hesitation our choice fell on dishy David Suchet and his lovely actress wife, Sheila. He'd played the lead in *Wedding Feast*, a production in which we first saw the talents of Miss McAuliffe. A good old nostalgia evening. Tanya insisted being in on this one.

Bought two whole fillet steaks, each of which I portioned into seven, knowing full well my children would arrive at dinner time to smell around for goodies. Everything can be prepared the day before and kept in the fridge. Cooked 2 large onions in butter with salt and pepper to taste. Placed a half slice of ham between each portion of steak. Brushed with generous helpings of brandy. Wrapped in tin foil. Could even cook and store mushrooms in the fridge. Likewise the vegies. Cleaned Jerusalem artichokes and cauliflower ready for cooking next day. Prepared fennel for braising. All into the fridge. Easy to cook and cover with simple white sauce next day. Great believer in being ahead of myself. Means I can enjoy the event, too!

My starter was to be *tsatziki* but not in the form usually served up. I grate my cucumber very coarsely and wrap it in muslin to drain out as much moisture as possible. And whereas I've found most restaurants give you a large proportion of yoghurt to cucumber, I give the reverse.

Dessert was a new discovery. Last week was invited by my friend Gunter Coenen to a wonderful dinner he'd cooked by himself. Quite a feat for the man who runs the Goethe Institute single-handed. He's being transferred to Paris. I'll miss him, and he'll miss London. Went alone. A. was in Leicester rehearsing *One More Ride*. For his

six guests Gunter had made a dessert consisting of layers of light
sponge biscuits soaked in Calvados with slices of apple poached in
cider slipped in between. The whole topped by piped cream. Takes
no time to make, looks impressive when presented, tastes delicious.

As usual I had to add my personal touch. Introduced ground
hazelnuts. Mistake. They soaked up the juice from the apple.
Fortunately the fresh strawberries I'd prepared as a side plate
provided the moisture. Everyone seemed satisfied. No room for
cheese. No left-overs either!

A. had taken off four days from rehearsing *One More Ride* in order
to be in on rehearsals of his radio play, *Bluey*, specially written for the
1984 European Radio Commission. Sorry not to have had a party for
that cast, but radio plays never seem an occasion. They're rehearsed
and over in three or four days. Perhaps I'll make one for them when it
goes out. To compensate, I baked them my chocolate rum raisin cake
for their tea on first day's rehearsal.

Nichola was one of the cast. Star-studded it was: Patrick Stewart,
David Swift, Joe Melia, Mary Wimbush and a host of radio actors
whom A. had not heard of but who he ecstatically announced were
'tremendous, moving, extraordinary! And they got their characters
at once. With no rehearsals. It's amazing!' And it is amazing, to get a
90-minute play rehearsed and recorded in only four days.

Recording scheduled to finish on Sunday evening at 7 p.m.
Instructed Nichola to make sure he rushed away at once to be home in
time for my dinner guests. Hard of me to take him away from
drinking with actors who'd just worked for his play, but a date is a
date! He needn't have troubled. Everyone was late. I'd prepared fillet
of beef in puff pastry. The beef had been half cooked and was now
rolled in the puff pastry awaiting a last twenty minutes of cooking.
Had everyone arrived at eight as invited, I'd have had ample time to
gauge the last twenty minutes. Ian and Sean came at around 8.30 and
Janet, who'd driven from her cottage in Suffolk, turned up at 9.15

full of exuberant spirits and apologies. I thrust a glass of champagne into her hand and pushed them all through to the dinning room. The beef was over-cooked.

A good party, however. 'But all those egos round the table!' observed my daughter. Magda joined us. As a young playwright, she had a right to a place with those actors. And of course I could show off my grand-daughter! Sean said he loved other people's houses so A. took him on a tour, ending up in his study crammed with almost a quarter of a century of accumulated books, files, manuscripts and theatrical memorabilia. As the Suchets left, David looked at the framed design of the Stockholm production of *The Merchant*. 'A marvellous play! I'd love to play it.' We'd always wanted him to play the Shylock role, if only someone would produce it! He added: 'You know what would make a fantastic project? To put on the whole trilogy – *The Jew Of Malta*, *The Merchant Of Venice*, and *The Merchant*. And I'd play them all!' A breathtaking concept. But who'd ever have the imagination and courage to do it?

Tsatziki (Cucumber in Yoghurt)

2 large cucumbers, sliced
1/2 pint / 300 ml Greek yoghurt
2 tablespoons fresh mint

2 cloves garlic, crushed
Salt and pepper to taste

Slice cucumber the day before. Wrap in a teacloth. Squeeze as much moisture out as possible. Leave in cloth, to enable remaining moisture to be absorbed. Mix yoghurt, chopped mint, crushed garlic, salt and pepper together with cucumber slices.

This is delicious on its own or with lamb.

Fillet of Beef in Puff Pastry

1 lb / 450 g puff pastry
1 fillet of beef
2 large onions
1/2 lb / 225 g mushrooms,
   chopped
2 oz / 50 g butter

1/2 lb / 225 g ham
Salt and lots of black
   pepper
1 tablespoon brandy
1 egg for glazing

Cut fillet into about 7 slices. Do not cut through completely. Put aside.

Fry onion and mushrooms in butter for 5 minutes. Put half slice of ham between each slice of fillet, together with some of the onion and mushroom mix. Season with salt and pepper. Pull fillet together and secure with skewers. Brush generously with brandy. Bake at 180°C / 350°F / gas mark 4 for 15 minutes. Leave to cool slightly. Wrap puff pastry around fillet. Cut pastry shapes to decorate top. Glaze with egg. Bake for further 15 minutes at 220°C / 425°F / gas mark 7.

Braised Fennel

4 fennel bulbs
¼ pint / 150 ml chicken stock
Juice of half a lemon

Salt and pepper to taste
1 oz / 25 g butter
1 tablespoon chopped parsley

Cut fennel lengthwise into 4 pieces and put in oven-dish with stock, lemon juice, and seasoning. Dot with butter. Cover and bake for 40 minutes at 190°C / 375°F / gas mark 5. Serve with chopped parsley.

Apple Calvados

1 lb / 450 g sponge finger
  biscuits
1 tablespoon Calvados
1 lb / 450 g Cox's Orange
  Pippin apples, peeled and
  sliced

¼ pint / 150 ml sweet cider
1 oz / 25 g castor sugar
½ pint / 300 ml double cream,
  whipped
½ teaspoon vanilla

Soak sponge fingers in Calvados. Place half of them in bottom of dish. Poach apples in cider and sugar till soft. Remove apples with slotted spoon, and layer over biscuits. (Throw cider away or drink!) Place remaining biscuits over apples. Leave to cool. Whip cream with vanilla and spread over top. Serve cold.

Why do first nights present me with problems? I suppose because so many of them take place in the provinces. *One More Ride On The Merry-Go-Round* opened at the Phoenix Arts Theatre in Leicester three nights ago. Friends, relatives, people coming in from various parts of the world, all needed to be chaperoned, dressed warmly and fed. Koichi Kimura, our director from Tokyo; Sara Sue Alexander, our 'woman' in Paris . . . Wanted so much to give our friends a decent meal, either on arrival or when the curtain came down. After

Sunday
28 April

all, they'd made the effort to get to Leicester. On these occasions there are always three main problems to deal with: transport, tickets, food. In the past, I've hired coaches, which with the price of provincial theatre seats and my free meal thrown in makes it a good, cheap night out. For Leicester I decided everyone must make their own way – the experience of guaranteeing a full coach and then having people ring to cancel at the last minute was too frustrating. Even so, had problems trying to fit people into other people's cars. It's a lot to expect drivers to travel back the same night.

The second problem is tickets. The box office has to be as patient with us as I have to be with wavering friends and relatives.

The third problem is the food. Not the preparation but the transporting of it and where it should be eaten. For the first night of *The Wedding Feast* in Leeds, I hired a coach and packed goodies only for the travellers, to whom I offered fare from baskets, walking up and down the aisle like Nell Gwyn. For the first night of *The Merchant* in Birmingham, management provided the drink but I hired a coach for 60 and transported food in the back to feed guests, actors and technicians. The corridors and offices of the Rep were strewn with goodies. I loved everyone's amazement.

This all seems natural to me. Effort has to be two-sided. But the Phoenix presented two other problems. I wanted to 'receive' those who'd made the effort to come to our first night; management understandably didn't want, as a matter of policy, to separate first night people into their people and ours. They too planned to lay on 'a little something, pizza and such', so they didn't want the cast seduced away to my feast table. They wanted them to mingle. Besides, I was warned, the word would soon get round that real food was on offer and it would be pounced upon before the actors could get to it. *That*, I understood. It had happened when I made food for the first night of *The Friends* in the Roundhouse. About 150 dropped out of the sky on to that spread and hardly anything was left for our poor, battered cast. (That whole period had been a nightmare. I'd made lunch for the actors every day for about four weeks – but that's another story.)

Keep getting diverted. Leicester! Not only didn't they want a separate event going on, there was no place to have it. But I *had* to feed my guests even if not the cast! We compromised. I'd feed them *before* the play began. They'd clear the Green Room for me, a place normally used for rehearsals, though during these days it was the place technicians were sleeping, as the set for *One More Ride* was complex and they were working on it, by rota, round the clock. Was there somewhere to heat the food? The front-of-house lady politely informed me their kitchen wasn't large enough to swing a cat around. (Poor cats! I've often wondered who'd ever want to do a thing like that anyway!)

So, heating was out of the question, the food had to be cold. What could I make that wouldn't spoil on a two-hour journey up the M1 in the back of my car? Fortunately experience taught there were masses of good, tasty things which could be transported in this fashion: fried chicken, salmon cutlets, fish balls, salads, quiches, cheeses, even cakes and desserts. It goes without saying (though one always *does* say it!) that all dishes and cutlery have to be disposable, because who wants to be left with dishes to wash? As usual, went to town on desserts. Made toasted coconut tart, honey cake and tassies. The tassies are a recipe passed on to me by my eighty-year-old American friend Mal, who still serves them at her drinks parties.

Fried Chicken

4 oz / 100 g flour
1 teaspoon paprika
Salt and pepper to taste
4 eggs

12 drumsticks
Pan of vegetable oil for deep frying

Mix flour and seasonings in bowl. Beat eggs. Dip drumsticks one at a time into flour, then the beaten eggs, and back into the flour. Allow oil to become hot but not too hot, because drumsticks must cook for 15 minutes in order to be cooked through. If the oil is too hot, the outside will burn before meat next the bone is cooked.

Salmon Cutlets

1 large tin red salmon
1 large Spanish onion, grated
2 eggs, beaten
1 oz / 25 g matzo meal or breadcrumbs
Salt and pepper to taste

1 teaspoon cinnamon
Pan of vegetable oil for deep frying

Mash salmon with fork. Add grated onion and beaten eggs, matzo meal, salt, pepper and cinnamon. Roll mixture into balls the size of egg. Heat oil, but not too hot. Deep fry for 10 minutes till golden brown.

Fish Balls

2 lb / 1 kg minced fish	2 oz / 50 g matzo meal
4 eggs	1 teaspoon castor sugar
2 large onions, grated	Salt and pepper to taste
1 oz / 25 g ground almonds	Vegetable oil for deep frying

Beat eggs. Add to minced fish. Fold in onions, ground almonds, matzo meal, sugar, salt and pepper. (I find fish requires more salt to bring out flavour.) Roll into balls size slightly smaller than an egg. Heat oil, not too hot. Deep fry for 15 minutes till golden brown.

Quiche Lorraine

1 lb / 450 g shortcrust pastry	1 tablespoon Parmesan, grated
1 medium onion, chopped	4 eggs, lightly beaten
1 tablespoon butter	½ pint / 300 ml single cream
½ lb / 225 g Gruyère cheese, grated	½ teaspoon nutmeg
	Salt and pepper to taste

Line a 10 in / 25 cm flan dish with shortcrust pastry. Fry onion in butter. Sprinkle onion and cheese evenly over pastry. Combine eggs, cream, nutmeg, salt and pepper, pour over onion and cheeese mixture. Bake at 200°C / 400°F / gas mark 6 for 15 minutes. Reduce heat to 180°C / 350°F / gas mark 4 and cook for further 30 minutes or until custard is set.

Coleslaw

1 medium white cabbage, finely shredded	½ large onion, chopped
1 medium cucumber, chopped	4 tablespoons wine vinegar
1 medium green pepper, chopped	2 tablespoons vegetable oil
1 large carrot, grated	1 tablespoon sugar
	1 tablespoon mayonnaise

Mix all ingredients and chill several hours before serving.

3 lb / 1.3 kg potatoes
2 tablespoons white wine
2 tablespoons vegetable oil
Salt and pepper to taste
2 tablespoons finely chopped
   onions

2 oz / 50 g toasted almonds
2 tablespoons finely chopped
   black olives
2 tablespoons mayonnaise

Cook potatoes slowly until tender. Don't overcook or dicing them will not be possible. When cool enough to handle, peel and dice into a deep bowl. Pour white wine over them. Gently mix in oil, salt, pepper and onions. Leave to cool. An hour before serving add almonds and olives. Bind with mayonnaise.

Savoury Almond Rice

8 oz / 225 g brown rice
1 oz / 25 g butter
1 medium onion, chopped
1 teaspoon turmeric
1 teaspoon cumin

1 pint / 600 ml chicken stock
Salt and pepper to taste
2 oz / 50 g flaked almonds
2 oz / 50 g raisins

Melt butter, fry onion. Stir in rice, turmeric, cumin, and cook for a few seconds. Pour in stock. Add salt and pepper. Bring to boil. Simmer for 45 minutes by which time stock should have been absorbed. Withdraw from heat. Toast almonds under grill till brown. Stir raisins and almonds into the rice and turn into bowl.

Can be eaten hot or cold. Because this was part of next day's moveable feast, I kept almonds and raisins in separate containers to add on arrival in Leicester, otherwise almonds would be soggy.

Toasted Coconut Tart

1 lb / 450 g shortcrust pastry
8 oz / 225 g desiccated coconut
6 eggs, separated
2 oz / 50 g sugar
1 oz / 25 g cornflour

Pinch of salt
1/2 pint / 300 ml milk
4 oz / 100 g butter
1 teaspoon vanilla

Line 10 in / 25 cm tin with shortcrust pastry (see page 13). Toast coconut in oven at 150°C / 300°F / gas mark 2 for 40 minutes. Beat egg yolks and sugar. Gradually add cornflour and salt. Bring milk to scalding point and add to egg yolk mix. Cook until thick. Remove from heat. Add butter. Beat egg whites and fold in 6 oz / 175 g coconut. Add vanilla. Pour into pastry crust. Sprinkle remaining 2 oz / 50 g of coconut on top. Bake at 190°C / 375°F / gas mark 5 until firm to touch, for about 40 minutes.

Honey Cake

1 teacup clear honey	6 oz / 175 g raisins
3 oz / 75 g sugar	1 level teaspoon baking powder
3 oz / 75 g butter, melted	8 oz / 225 g flour
2 eggs	1 teaspoon cinnamon

Grease loaf tin. Hand whisk honey, sugar and butter. Add eggs, one by one, beating in between. Mix in raisins, baking powder, flour and cinnamon to make even consistency. Pour into greased loaf tin. Bake at 190°C / 375°F / gas mark 5 for about 40 minutes until firm.

Do not cut until next day.

Tassies

I recommend you make these as bite-sized tarts because they are very rich.

Pastry

¼ lb / 100 g butter	4 oz / 100 g flour
3 oz / 75 g cream cheese	

Blend these three ingredients. Roll into walnut-sized balls. Leave to chill for 15 minutes. Press pastry balls into *petits-fours* tins to make shells.

Filling

2 eggs, beaten	½ teaspoon vanilla
1½ tablespoons brown sugar	¼ lb / 100 g pecans, crushed
1 tablespoon melted butter	

Mix together these ingredients. Fill pastry shells. Bake for 20 minutes at 180°C / 350°F / gas mark 4.

Summertime approaches. New tasks stare me in the face! A. and I share the duties of this house. He thinks the thinking and I do the doing. The garden, for instance. That's mine as well as the kitchen. And the grass has started to grow again. For many years I've run this house single-handed. Occasionally I succumb to my husband's insistence and hire help. But no one's ever as thorough or as fast as I am. Can't blame them. It's not their house. What love can they have for it?

I love my garden. It's not a sightseeing garden. Nothing spectacular lives there, but I keep it trimmed and tidy and it's a pleasure for friends and family to sit out in the hot days. This morning I was out there pottering, thinking about my dinner party on the 5th May, and forthcoming parties. So many friends to whom I owe hospitality. What delights I dreamt up to cook for them!

Decided Sunday nights are good for dinner parties, especially for theatre friends. On the other hand they're not so good for people who flee to the countryside for weekends. Have to juggle a great deal. Also with A.'s comings and goings. Love having him at the other end of my dinner table. He's my best critic! Also need him to bring up and uncork wines. He doesn't really know much about them but he's trying to build up a cellar. Afraid we're not very careful with our amounts. Have you ever been to a dinner party where the host keeps the decanter on the sideboard and only fills your small glass when *they* remember to get up and serve you? We leave ours on the table. Guests can help themselves if we forget. Believe in plenty. People normally can judge their limits. Though not always! Often worry about guests who've reeled through our squeaky front gate. It's not funny . . .

Feeling harassed. Six guests tonight but I've just had a day full of comings and goings. Pause to write this between the last coming that's gone and the six who are to come. Thank God I organised their food yesterday!

The day began with Graeme Watkins flying in from Leicester for breakfast at 10.30 to report to A. on the full houses for *One More Ride*. Local reviews were superlative, word of mouth is strong and a few London managements are coming up, so everyone's exhilarated. Problem is that London theatres are full and there's a queue of shows waiting to get into town. A tour is being planned, rather like an aeroplane having to circle before it can land. God! We need this transfer. A. moans: 'I'm tired of being famous, I want just one commercial success as well!' Two savage reviews had appeared in the national press, written by a couple of second-stringers. One producer had said that, because of them, he couldn't see it was worth making the journey to see the play for himself. A. knew him and wanted to write him a letter of rebuke for being lazy and gullible. Graeme talked him out of it while I cooked him a breakfast of grilled sausages, tomatoes, fried eggs and toast.

As Graeme left, a young Roumanian from the World Service arts programme, Meridian, came to interview A. about *One More Ride*. Served him fresh coffee and some left-over apple strudel I'd made during the week. And as they came down from the study, our Norwegian friends walked in.

Anne Gulestad is an actress who long ago directed *The Kitchen* in Bergen. She runs a touring company which took a production of *Roots* round the fjords some years back. We were invited to accompany them. One of the happiest holidays I've ever had. Love Scandinavia. Have a special feeling for the area. Coming from Norfolk, it could be that I'm the product of an ancient Viking rape! One of my dreams is to join in the rounding-up of the reindeer in Lapland.

Anne here with actress daughter, Agnetta, and lawyer husband, Wilhelm, for just three days to take part in a memorial for a writer, Harvard Elvin, who'd translated a lot of Norwegian writing into English. Wanted to take us out to lunch, but – oh, I don't know, seemed so much easier and friendlier to get us all round the kitchen table. (Couldn't use the dining room table, that was all set up!) Magda, Lindsay and Tanya there too. And of course the adorable Natasha.

If you're curious about how I fed seven at lunch as well as preparing for eight in the evening, well – when I know I'm going to have a heavy weekend like this, I prepare as far ahead as possible. Two days ago I marinated chicken portions in a mixture of garlic, fresh soya sauce, tabasco, Worcester sauce, tomato purée, honey and ginger. Turned the pieces over from time to time. All that was needed was to grill them. (Slowly, or the marinade burns.) Mixed, stir-fried vegetables and salad are easy to do at the last minute. Made a simple dessert: hot creamy rice pudding with a topping of mixed nuts and hot cherry sauce. That was lunch. For dinner: made the starter easy for myself by baking a blind pastry case on Saturday ready for a hot asparagus tart. Asparagus are in season. Can never resist them. A guest, Aida Young, chose the main meal. Bumped into her at a preview of *Pravda* and asked was there any meat she preferred. Veal, she said. *Osso buco*, I decided, another easy dish to think about for my hectic weekend. Half cooked it on Saturday. Will need only to pop it in the oven for about two hours before eating. Even made the dessert ahead of time: mango mousse with piped cream. Found a handy new tool, an orange peel stripper. No problem to cover mousse with thin strips of tangy peel and serve straight from the fridge. I watched with incredulity as A. ate his huge lunch after his huge breakfast and before the huge dinner I'd prepared. He's so engaged in conversation he doesn't seem to notice what he puts away.

Brandy in the lounge. Wilhelm fell asleep and snored loudly, much to the embarrassment of his family. We enjoyed it. Meant he felt relaxed. Wished we could do it ourselves! Anne has been invited to take over running the theatre in Bergen. Norway's oldest. She's hesitating. We urged her to accept. 'Will you write a new play for us?' she asks. A. replies he's drained, but offers to come and direct *Caritas* which the three Scandinavian touring theatres commissioned four years ago and never performed, thinking it was too difficult for their rural audiences!

They'd been to see their old friend Liv Ullman, in the Pinter revival of *Old Times*. 'The Norwegian press give her a rough time,' they told us. Familiar story! They ended the afternoon in the study listening to the recording made by Sheila Steafel of A.'s half-hour play which he wrote for her, *Yardsale*.

Left at 4.30, so I can put my feet up. Well, not really. I'm writing this!

Marinated Chicken

8 chicken pieces, breast or leg, skinned	1 tablespoon sherry
	1 tablespoon honey
1 oz / 25 g fresh ginger, grated	1 tablespoon Worcestershire
2 generous cloves of garlic, crushed	sauce
	2 tablespoons tomato purée
3 tablespoons soya sauce	1 teaspoon tabasco

Mix all ingredients in a bowl. (I like to keep a jar of this marinade in the fridge. It's good for pork chops, too!)

Lay skinned chicken pieces in marinade overnight. Throughout next day, before cooking, turn them over as often as possible.

To cook: lay pieces in grill pan. Grill gently for 30 minutes, turning them after 15 minutes.

Creamed Rice Pudding with Hot Cherry Sauce

4 tablespoons rice	1 egg white
1 pint / 600 ml milk	¼ pint / 150 ml double cream
1 vanilla pod	1 tablespoon toasted almonds
2 tablespoons castor sugar	

Simmer rice in milk, with vanilla pod, for approximately two hours or until it is soft. Add sugar and turn into a bowl to cool. Remove vanilla pod. Whip cream until stiff. Whip egg white separately, then fold cream and egg white together. Mix gently into rice. Top with almonds. Serve with hot cherry sauce.

Cherry sauce

Large tin morello cherries	1 dessertspoon arrowroot

Tip cherries and juice into saucepan. Extract tablespoon of juice. Use this to make paste with arrowroot. Pour paste into saucepan. Heat cherries, juice and paste till thick, stirring all the time. Serve hot cherry sauce on the side of each portion of rice.

Monday 6 May

Sunday night dinner party included Bob Gavron and his new partner, Kate; Aida and Gideon Young; Catherine Freeman; Zena Walker. Bob's one of our oldest friends. Indebted to him for helping us through bad times. Kate's production director at Heinemann's. Daniel travelled to Leicester with them for the first night of *One More Ride* and had talked about his approach to photography and how he admired the work of Fay Godwin. Kate had remembered and brought a copy of Heinemann's edition of her photographs. Bob, who's recently bought the Folio Society, brought the Society's latest edition of Somerset Maugham's short stories. He runs the St Ives printing works and has much in common with Gideon Young, also a printer. Aida is a film producer. Worked with A. on his film adaptation of 'The Wesker Trilogy', another unmade project! Can't remember how we met Catherine! Seem to have known her for ages.

She's head of BBC TV documentaries. A. was on one of her afternoon women's programmes. To do with depression. I remember him looking out of place with the real depressives. Zena had played Phoebe in A.'s production of Osborne's *The Entertainer* for Theatre Clwyd – the only time he's ever directed another writer's play. Lovely production. None of the national critics went up to see it.

But no one said anything about the food! I never know whether to interpret that as a successful event – everyone's too engrossed with everyone else to say anything – or not. I muttered 'failure' to A. who said 'Nonsense! A great success.' Not sure I can ever tell though despite the talking, they cleaned their plates!

Hot Asparagus Tart

This is made exactly as quiche Lorraine (see p. 42), substituting the cheese with the tips of 2 bunches of asparagus which have been steamed for 10 minutes in lightly salted water.

Osso Buco

5 lb / 2.26 kg knuckle of veal	2 tablespoons flour
2 tablespoons vegetable oil	½ pint / 300 ml white wine
1 oz / 25 g butter	2 chicken stock cubes
6 carrots, sliced	1 pint / 600 ml water
4 sticks celery, sliced	Salt and pepper to taste
2 onions, sliced	1 sprig parsley, finely chopped
2 cloves of garlic, crushed	Grated rind of one lemon

Boil water and dissolve stock cubes.

Fry veal pieces in heavy-bottomed pan in oil and butter. Take out and lay on kitchen paper to absorb fat. Put chopped vegetables into pan, fry in remaining fat. Stir in flour to make roux. Let out with wine and chicken stock. Season with salt and pepper. Return veal to sauce, cover with lid. Cook for about 3 hours on low heat. Before serving, sprinkle lemon rind and parsley on the top.

For me, this is the tastiest way to eat veal.

Mango Mousse with Tangy Orange Peel

(For tangy orange peel, see page 16.)

5 mangoes, peeled
1 oz / 25 g gelatine
6 tablespoons of lime juice
4 oz / 100 g granulated sugar

6 tablespoons double cream
2 egg whites
Pinch of salt

Dissolve gelatine in lime juice. Purée mango flesh in blender. Add lime juice and gelatine. Add sugar. Whip cream until thick. Fold into mousse mixture. Whip egg whites with pinch of salt until stiff. Fold into mousse mixture. Pour into large dish and leave to set in fridge for about 3 hours. When set, sprinkle tangy orange peel on top.

Wednesday *15 May* When I told a friend I was making a dinner for my Gemini friends (A.'s birthday is 24th May, Tanya is 25th, I'm the 30th) she asked: 'What do Geminis eat?' Made me wish I could invent two of everything. Instead, I'll bake dishes as memorable as possible. Spoil the Geminis!

One of them, Jill Tweedie, wrote asking 'Can I bring my other half? In this case I mean the other half of *me*.' I was thrown at first, not knowing whether she was making a Gemini joke or asking in a roundabout way whether she could bring her husband, Alan Brien. Played safe and checked. She was referring to Alan. Had to tell her it was for real Geminis only. 'That's absolutely fine by me,' she laughed. Ladies are in the majority, sixteen out of eighteen.

Every year my party grows a little. Birth signs invariably crop up in all kinds of unlikely conversations so I keep discovering new Geminis.

This year I'll have the additional work for Tanya's party on the 25th. Though I'm pleased to say she's persuaded a friend to let her hold it in his house. Still, there's 25 to cook for in her gathering, 18 in mine on the 26th – it's going to take me two days of preparation I can see. No short cuts with mammoth dishes of cottage pie. The kids are now sophisticated connoisseurs. The food has to be special!

Will do my shopping on Thursday which will then give me those two days for preparation. After that Daniel has to take the car to Wales to pick up A. who's been at work in the cottage. Feel guilty leaving him on his own with no transport, but once he's up in them hills, isolated, he never wants to move anyway. As for my dinner on the 26th, well, you know very often I don't decide what to make until I go out and see what looks good. Frequently I come home with two different things and don't make up my mind until the last minute. Whatever is rejected – if anything is ever rejected in this house where there's always a hungry mouth – I freeze it. Not the mouth, I hasten to add!

Am tempted to cook pigeons. Haven't had them since I was a kid. They make something a little out of the ordinary. But risky. So perhaps a fresh salmon.

Rehearsals begin today for *The Merchant* in Germany. They've called it *Shylock*. Wonder how it'll be received *there*?

Knock on front door caught me in the middle of cooking and general household chores. Was trying a new recipe for duck. Wanted to take it to my mum. Visiting her tomorrow for a couple of days in Norfolk. She's passionate about duck. Rarely gets to eat it. Wasn't really a new recipe. Just that I'd made it a few weeks ago and had forgotten what I'd done! Had to do it again and make notes this time.

Thursday 16 May

The knocker was Sybil Robinson, lecturer in English from Wisconsin University. A couple of years ago she was involved in a TV project to make a series under the heading 'Man and Woman' for which *The Four Seasons* was to be the pilot project. It never happened. The company with whom they'd set up the first deal went bust six weeks later. When I think of the running around I did to help it to get off the ground. A. was directing John Osborne's *The Entertainer* in Clwyd. His TV adaptation of *The Four Seasons* was set in our house in the Black Mountains, so I drove Sybil and her producer friend there first, then up through twisting roads to North Wales to visit him in Clwyd. Then back to London after an overnight stay. 'Couldn't we have got a plane part of the way?' the producer asked. Poor Americans. Crazy days.

Sybil's here on a refresher course for the Alexander Technique (she's directing *Macbeth* with her students) which is taking place round the corner in Highgate. She'd rung me. I'd not had time to ring back. Felt guilty. Sat having coffee. She told me of the miserable hotel in Kensington she'd been booked into. I'd bought some biscuits for a cheesecake I'd been planning. Asked could she have one. 'I've not had lunch.' Invited her to stay at Bishops Road. All that waste on hotel bills and train fares from the other side of London!

Went to John Lewis to buy A.'s birthday present which I was sharing with the kids. We agreed that what the old man absolutely needed was an exercise bike. He goes to the study every day and gets no exercise other than running up and down stairs for coffee – or whatever other excuse he can find to break away. Worries me. Must add, in honesty, the thought had crossed my mind that I might use it too. So many people's birthdays in May – a heavy month – I can be forgiven for being just a little calculating.

Friday
17 May

Returned from hairdressers to find Sybil waiting on the doorstep to move in. Packed a few things for Norfolk trip. Left Sybil in the house. She was leaving for Scotland that night 'to soak up the atmosphere'. Called on Magda to deliver baby clothes I'd washed, and to dose myself up with enough Natasha-cuddles to last me the weekend. Realised that, damn! I'd forgotten my poor ole mum's duck in the fridge. Too late to return.

4 duck breasts   1 tablespoon honey
2 oz / 50 g flour   ½ pint / 300 ml chicken stock
Salt and pepper to taste   4 oz / 100 g fresh raspberries
1 oz / 25 g butter

Mix flour, salt and pepper. Coat duck pieces in flour mix. Using deep pan, fry breasts in butter until brown. Add honey and stock. Cook for 10 minutes, covered. Remove duck pieces and keep hot. Add raspberries to remaining juices and heat through. Sieve to remove the raspberry pips. Cut breasts into thin slices just before serving. Arrange on platter, cover with sauce.

Up early, to leave Norfolk for Bishops Road in time to get that duck *Sunday* out of the fridge and cook it for lunch for the kids. Usually return *19 May* laden with fresh vegetables but nothing out yet. Had to make do with fresh eggs and an old frying-pan I picked up for 50p in a jumble sale. One of my joys, jumble sales. First thing I ask Mum when I get through the door: 'Got any jumble sales lined up for us?'

Trips home are packed with events which I plan to get her out of her house and lonely existence – whist drives, visits to the sea, trips round the narrow lanes filled with houses and manors about which she seems to know everything. This time took her to Watton for an evening of one-act plays. Local amateurs in competition. Last year Radio Norfolk organised 'An Arnold Wesker Week' (he's the only playwright to have written three plays in Norfolk dialect) and one of the staff asked if she could present *Four Portraits*, his one-act play for an actress, at the Watton event. She did not win a prize! But Mum sat eyes glued to the stage. 'Sooner see this live acting any time than that ole rubbish they give out on the box.'

The first of my brood in were L.J. and Magda. 'Food! Food!' my eldest called out. I baby-sat while they went to the movies.

The birthdays are upon me. Spent some of yesterday and this morning shopping for the busy weekend ahead. Packed Daniel off in the car to pick up A. at the Welsh cottage. He's working and recovering from reviews of *One More Ride*. Not that he reads the bad ones. I have to suffer reading those and warn him to avoid them. What has depressed him most is not that two reviews in national papers were bad (savage, actually, he does seem to attract a special wrath), but that they've deterred managements from going up to see the play for themselves. He can't understand why they would take notice of two second-stringers rather than give him, after all these years, the benefit of the doubt, just to have a look! *Distinctions*, his new collection of lectures and journalism, came out on the same day *One More Ride* opened, and a critic of that had written: 'I think Mr Wesker over-estimates the influence of critics.' They just have no idea. Actually, *I* found it much more outrageous that all the Sunday newspapers ignored the play while the *Observer* sent their critic to the other theatre in Leicester to review a seventeenth-century play which was coming to London anyway!

Somehow, though, he finds energy to bounce back. Ring him every evening at 6.30 to bring him up to date with the day's news. The other evening he told me with great excitement that he'd written the book for a musical of his first play, *The Kitchen*. Here we go again! Can't bear these ups and downs. Don't know about him but it's slowly killing me!

Anyway, packed up some fried fish for Daniel to take for the dieting old man of the mountains, and some veal escalopes with matzo meal for Daniel to fry for himself. Am worried. It's the first time he's ever driven a long journey alone. Also sent along some of A.'s birthday cards – his is tomorrow – and Tanya's present to him: a set of six different-coloured coffee cups. Nothing can stop the plotting and planning.

Tanya put in an order to me for her birthday party: mostly salads. Together we worked out a menu: chicken fruit salad; saffron rice with mixed vegetables; potato salad in sour cream and chopped onions; Waldorf salad (which couldn't really be called that because Daniel doesn't like walnuts and so I had to use cashews instead, sacrilege for the celery and apples, I know); chicken and mushroom crêpes was the hot dish. For dessert we agreed on one of my trifles, a walnut tart and a cheesecake.

Boiled four chickens which provided me with some very concentrated stock. Might use it for *vichyssoise* later so I'll freeze it for now. Stripped flesh from the bones to keep in the fridge until Saturday when I'll make the chicken salad. Boiled lovely new potatoes for the second salad. Peeled, chopped and wept my way through about 2 lb of onions. Had the idea of using the chicken livers as stuffing for my pigeons. Fried them with lots of onion, salt, pepper and some seasoned breadcrumbs. All these little jobs save time, and who knows, if I get well ahead with my preparations, I'll have more time to devote to my grand-daughter at the weekend.

And the damn grass has grown again. Had to do that little chore today so that the 'back yard' will look tidy for the party days. Hard work, that, pushing and pulling the Flymo and then raking up all the cuttings. Still, good exercise, I tell myself. And then there's the pleasure of looking at a lush and well-groomed garden.

A. rang from the Groucho Club. He's joined a club for the first time in his life. Just opened, for writers and people in the media. Thought he'd call in there to look it over rather than come back to Bishops Road and then rush out again to do an interview at the BBC with John Dunn. Terrible interview! I hate listening to him on those shows. He's too open, and they jump in with their digs and jibes and he never knows how to answer them. Wish he'd stop giving interviews for ever. But he worries that to decline would seem arrogant.

Friday 24 May

Think I know what I'm cooking for the Gemini party.

Concentrated on finishing the salads and desserts for Tanya's party which they'll take over to Nick's house. Daniel's friend has kindly offered his place as the venue. Worked on the Gemini party too. Will spoil them with desserts. Have concocted something in place of a birthday cake. A monster thing using kiwis and strawberries. Wanted to use blackcurrants but had also made blackcurrant tarts. Daniel said: 'Don't do that! If you've got a whole plate of blackcurrant tarts you don't want another dish to taste of the same thing, do you?' He added: 'Blimey, Mum, it's a bit big, isn't it? You won't be able to pick it up with your hands.' Reminded him of the lovely huge helpings we got in Serendipity's in New York. He was right about the blackcurrants though.

Saturday 25 May

A. drove Sybil and Pamela Howard to Leicester for last night of *One More Ride*. Full, enthusiastic house. Cast angry and gloomy that it was over – it deserved to go on somewhere else. Story of our life!

Chicken Fruit Salad

1 lb / 450 g cooked chicken meat
½ cucumber, diced
2 oz / 50 g fresh ginger, grated
6 spring onions, chopped
1 sprig parsley, chopped
2 Cox's Orange Pippins,
  peeled and diced

½ lb / 225 g grapes, mixed white and black, halved and pipped
¼ lb / 100 g sultanas, pre-washed

Chop chicken. Mix with above ingredients.

Dressing

1 tablespoon vegetable oil
1 tablespoon vinegar
1 dessertspoon sugar

1 teaspoon French mustard
1 clove garlic, crushed

Mix dressing ingredients. Pour over chicken salad.

Saffron Rice with Mixed Vegetables

4 rashers of bacon
8 oz / 225 g long grain rice,
  cooked
1 medium onion, chopped
1 oz / 25 g butter
Pinch of saffron dissolved in
  dessertspoon of boiling water
Salt and pepper to taste

8 oz / 225 g packet garden peas
8 oz / 225 g packet mixed green and red peppers, chopped
8 oz / 225 g packet diced carrots
½ pint / 300 ml water

Grill bacon until crisp, then chop. Add bacon to cooked rice. Fry chopped onion in butter till brown. Add cooked rice, bacon and dissolved saffron to pan of onions. Salt and pepper to taste. Put pan aside.

Boil vegetables together in water for 10 minutes. Mix with rice and pile on platter.

Potato Salad with Sour Cream

2 lb / 900 g potatoes
2 eggs, hard boiled and chopped
1 large onion, chopped
2 tablespoons vegetable oil

½ pint / 300 ml sour cream
1 dessertspoon French mustard
1 teaspoon vinegar

Boil potatoes and cut into slices. Mix potatoes, eggs and chopped onion together. Combine sour cream with French mustard, vinegar and oil. Pour over potato mix. Stir carefully not to break potatoes.

Waldorf Salad

1 large head of celeriac
1 lb / 450 g walnuts, chopped
8 oz / 225 g white grapes,
    pipped
2 Cox's Orange Pippins, diced

Juice of 1 lemon
4 tablespoons of mayonnaise
Salt and pepper to taste
Chives to garnish

Peel celeriac. Cut into cubes and boil until tender. Mix with chopped walnuts, grapes and apples in a salad bowl. Make dressing of mayonnaise, lemon juice, salt and pepper. Add to salad, mixing lightly. Garnish with chives.

Chicken and Mushroom Crêpes (serves 12 to 15)

Crêpes

4 eggs, separated
4 tablespoons plain flour
Pinch of salt

1 pint / 600 ml milk
2 oz / 50 g butter
Greaseproof paper

Mix flour, egg yolks and salt. Add milk until mixture is smooth. Just before using whip egg whites until stiff and add to mixture.

Grease pan well with butter. Fry pancakes both sides, keeping as thin as possible. Stack with greaseproof paper between each one.

Filling

2 oz / 50 g mushrooms, sliced
1 oz / 25 g butter
1 oz / 25 g flour
½ pint / 300 ml chicken stock

6 oz / 175 g cooked chicken,
    chopped
Salt and pepper to taste

Fry mushrooms in butter. Remove from pan with slotted spoon, leaving fat behind. Add flour to make roux. Let out with stock to make sauce. Return mushrooms to sauce. Add chicken and seasoning.

Fill the crêpes, carefully tucking in the sides so as no filling escapes. Roll up and lay in oblong dish, covering with any remaining sauce. Put in oven at 200°C / 400°F / gas mark 6 for 10 minutes.

Trifle

1 packet sponge cakes	2 fresh mangoes, sliced
½ pint / 300 ml raspberry sauce	1 pint / 600 ml double cream,
2 bananas, sliced	whipped
1 pint / 600 ml custard	8 oz / 225 g toasted almonds

Custard

4 egg yolks	1 pint / 600 ml milk
1 teaspoon cornflour	1 teaspoon vanilla
2 tablespoons castor sugar	

You can use packet custard, but I prefer to make my own.

Beat egg yolks, cornflour, and sugar together. Bring milk to the boil and pour over mixture. Transfer to double boiler. Cook over low heat, until mixture coats wooden spoon. Add vanilla.

Raspberry sauce

8 oz / 225 g mashed raspberries	2 level teaspoons cornflour
2 tablespoons redcurrant jelly	1 tablespoon cold water

Heat raspberries and redcurrant jelly until jelly has dissolved. Blend cornflour with water. Add to raspberries. Stir mixture until thick. Pass through sieve to remove pips.

Place sponge cakes at bottom of large glass dish (it's attractive to see the layers). Cover with raspberry sauce. Make next layer of sliced banana. Pour over it pint of custard. If custard is still warm allow it to cool before laying down slices of fresh mango. Cover all with whipped cream. Scatter toasted almonds on top.

For an alcoholic variation, you can soak your sponge cakes in sherry, or Marsala, or whatever you wish.

Walnut Tart

½ lb / 225 g shortcrust pastry

Line 10 in / 25 cm tin with pastry. Bake blind at 200°C / 400°F / gas mark 6 for 15 minutes.

Filling

3 eggs
9 fl oz / 250 ml corn syrup
2 oz / 50 g brown sugar

4 oz / 100 g walnuts, chopped
Pinch of salt

Beat eggs slightly. Add all other ingredients, one by one, stirring continuously. Pour into pastry shell. Bake at 190°C / 375°F / gas mark 5 for 45 minutes.

Gemini party has come and gone. Was pleased with the way it turned out. Think everyone else was, too. Thank goodness I organise well ahead. Means I can cope with all eventualities – unexpected callers or last-minute problems.

*Sunday
26 May*

Such as: an Israeli friend, Llana Baniel, called in after lunch time. Her husband, Eran, is a writer and head of Israeli Radio drama. He's also just been appointed dramaturge of the Habima Theatre. They've bought the rights for *The Old Ones* and *The Merchant*. A. got him involved with working on the Koestler TV scripts. Llana came to tell us of a nightmare story in which the film company refused to pay Eran. They had to call in a top lawyer at great expense. One of the producers had turned up at their flat and, Llana related, 'he screamed lies and threats, in *our* flat in front of our children. I told Eran I'd be prepared to sell my house to pay lawyers to get satisfaction from them.' No one really appreciates the nightmares facing writers.

Fifteen of us sat down for dinner. Vera, an old friend and journalist, had insisted on bringing Jonathan, her son and one of A.'s godchildren. 'I'm terrified of leaving him alone,' she explained. 'But he's fifteen years old,' I said. 'I hate partings,' she replied. He's a lovely boy but he's not a Gemini so couldn't sit at the table. Sat upstairs instead watching TV, happier no doubt. She worried about him throughout the meal. Was he being fed enough? In addition to serving at table I found myself running up and down stairs too.

Greeted people with champagne and *cassis*. Ran out of *cassis*. Sometimes fall down on the details!

Must say I felt proud of the blue and white table layout. A. said: 'You'd think I was a commercially successful playwright!' There were all the sighs and oohs I enjoy. And this is what I offered them:

For starters, a chicken terrine (there must be a way of cooking it so that it slices better, will work on it! Not that it stopped them cleaning their plates!); quails eggs which, curiously, only a few sampled, wonder why?; fried fish balls, they made a good impression on those; and mackerel pâté. Only A. attacked that.

Everyone seemed bubbly and conversation flowed. Vera, who'd translated Nachum Goldman's autobiography from German for Weidenfeld's, was able to talk to Alex, a Weidenfeld editor, about why Goldman's son had cancelled publication of the book. Jill and Maxine discussed the plight of women in Latin American countries. Jill angry that women were being intimidated into contraceptive practices. Maxine trying to explain why. Now that *One More Ride* was over, Pauline Yates was able to discuss with her playwright what she thought had gone wrong with the production in which she'd played (wonderfully) a lead. Every part of the table was full of clinking cutlery and eager voices. Daniel called for a pause because, he claimed, the diners had eaten so much of the starters they'd never last out the dinner!

Went on to pigeons and fresh salmon. Had to get A. to 'pray silence for your hostess' so that I could inform them: 'Not more than nine of you can want pigeon 'cos that's all I've cooked. But if you all want fresh salmon, fine! 'cos I've got plenty of that.' After a lot of indecision I'd finally made it with cucumber sauce. Seven took pigeon. That meant Lindsay Joe could have one when he returned. (He'd gone to his office, he can't bear hanging around doing nothing, which is what sitting at a dinner table means for him.) The pigeon turned out a much stronger-tasting meat than I remembered from my childhood when mum used to make it into pies. Of course the red wine in which I braised it gave the meat an additional flavour. Made baby new potatoes, cauliflower, courgettes and *haricots verts*. Can't help it, love lots of different vegetables. Just enough so they had a taste of each.

Asked Tanya to read aloud from an amusing book I'd come across describing typical Gemini characteristics of the male and female.

Cause of wry and reflective laughter. My over-eager daughter went on to read other passages to do with the sun rising and the moon setting which turned the laughter into moans of confusion. Had to abandon that smartish.

Was indulgently over the top with my desserts. Three plates of little individual fruit tarts filled with blackcurrants, cherries and mandarin oranges over dollops of *crème patissière*; the tall four-layered cake; and a crêpe cake. Sold lots of portions of that – very light and tasty, having been soaked in Grand Marnier and heated.

Like serving coffee at the dinner table – everyone always seems so comfortable round it – but A. kept pointing out that guests like to change talking partners at least once in an evening, or be given the chance to. So, gave them one cup with their dessert and told them if they wanted second cups they'd find more in the lounge.

Had to get to the lounge sooner or later anyway because I'd asked Daniel to take a pyramid photograph. The 'pyramids' have become a feature of our holidays in the Welsh cottage. Those who share the holiday have to kneel and stand on each other, clustered in the space where the front gate opens, and be photographed as a record of their stay. Couldn't miss out on a Gemini group. I bought everyone a little birthday present, nothing much, a memento, and made them each clutch it as they formed their pyramid in front of the lounge fireplace. Promised everyone a copy of the photograph.

A. asked Sheila (Steafel) to do her skit 'Married to God' which never fails to convulse us. She followed this with her savage South African send-up called 'Kitty', impersonating a South African white middle-class lady who was being 'nice' about her black maid. An ironic piece in which she gives herself away by the dreadful patronising things she says of the maid. Magda, my black daughter-in-law, missed the irony and was offended by the patronising insults. Daniel and Tanya also felt it too near the knuckle. There's something worrying if the young can't accommodate irony.

All ended by describing surprise parties we'd organised or been part of. At the door Jill said she and Alan had been looking for a cottage to rent in Wales. By coincidence we'd heard of one very beautiful place in the Black Mountains near us. Promised Jill I'd phone for particulars. Marrying people to houses is almost as satisfying as marrying them to food!

Chicken Terrine

4 chicken breasts, minced raw
1½ lb / 650 g courgettes
1 bunch watercress, chopped
½ pint / 300 ml double cream

1 teaspoon rosemary, chopped
Salt and black pepper to taste
3 egg whites, whipped
1 large onion, chopped

Line a medium terrine with foil.

Cook courgettes for 5 minutes. Purée together with watercress, cream, rosemary and seasoning. Fold in whipped egg white. Fry chopped onion in butter and add to it the minced raw chicken.

Now put alternative layers of creamy mixture and chicken mixture in terrine until level with top. End with creamy mix. Cover with lid or tin foil. Stand in pan of water. Bake at 190°C / 375°F / gas mark 5 for one hour. Leave to cool overnight.

Mackerel Pâté

2 large smoked mackerel
3 oz / 75 g cream cheese
Juice of 1 lemon
2 cloves garlic, crushed

4 oz / 100 g butter, melted
Salt and pepper to taste
1 sprig parsley, chopped

Purée mackerel skinned and flaked, with other ingredients in blender. Transfer to dish. Garnish with parsley. Serve with hot toast.

Pigeon in Red Wine with Stuffing – for 8

4 pigeons, cleaned thoroughly
2 oz / 50 g butter
2 medium onions, chopped
4 oz / 100 g mushrooms, chopped

½ bottle red wine
¼ pint / 150 ml chicken stock
Salt and pepper to taste
1 oz / 25 g cornflour

Stuffing

1 oz / 25 g butter
1 large onion, chopped
2 tablespoons raisins
2 oz / 50 g split almonds
4 apricots, cooked and chopped

Grated rind and juice of 1 lemon
1 tablespoon parsley, chopped
Salt and pepper

Make stuffing first. Melt butter, fry onion until golden brown. Add raisins, almonds and apricots. Continue to fry for a few minutes. Transfer to bowl. Pour lemon juice and rind over it. Add parsley and seasoning. Mix well. Stuff into cavity of pigeons.

Now the pigeon. Using heavy-bottomed deep casserole, melt butter. Brown the stuffed pigeons, turning constantly. Remove pigeons. Add onions and mushrooms to butter. Fry for about 5 minutes. Add wine, stock and seasoning. Return pigeons to pot. Cover and simmer for 40 minutes. Remove pigeons. Keep hot. Take a tablespoon of liquid and make into a paste with cornflour. Add paste to liquid to thicken. Ladle sauce over pigeons.

Delicious served with creamed potatoes and mangetouts. If you halve the pigeons before serving them, you'll save your guests from having to wrestle with them.

Poached Salmon with Cucumber Sauce

6 lb / 2.75 kg salmon	1 bay leaf
1½ pints / 900 ml water	1 tablespoon sea salt
½ pint / 300 ml white wine	Black pepper to taste
2 sprigs of parsley	

Use all above ingredients to poach salmon in fish kettle for 30 minutes. Remove salmon from kettle. Keep warm. Freeze fish stock for future use.

Cucumber sauce

1 large cucumber, peeled and grated	1 dessertspoon dried tarragon
¼ pint / 150 ml double cream	Salt and pepper to taste

Beat cream until thick. Add chopped tarragon. Season to taste. Just before serving, mix in grated cucumber.

In Place of a Birthday Cake

This cake, a chocolate sponge, came about because I'd been making fruit tarts for Gemini party and had a lot of fruit left over. Decided to make a cake to use them up.

Chocolate sponge

3 oz / 75 g self-raising flour
2 level tablespoons drinking
  chocolate
3 large eggs, separated

4 oz / 100 g castor sugar
2 tablespoons hot water
1 oz / 25 g butter, melted
½ teaspoon vanilla

Grease two 8 in / 20 cm sandwich tins.

Mix flour and chocolate powder. Whisk egg whites. Beat egg yolks with sugar. Mix hot water and melted butter with vanilla. Pour into egg and sugar mixture. Fold in flour and chocolate. Fold in egg whites. Divide mixture between two tins. Bake at 190°c / 375°F / gas mark 5 for 25 minutes.

When cool, slice each cake in two to make 4 layers.

Filling

2 tablespoons Crème de Cacao
Crème patissière (see page 31)
4 tablespoons double cream

3 kiwi fruit, peeled and sliced
½ lb / 225 g fresh strawberries,
  sliced

Sprinkle Crème de Cacao over each of the 4 layers of chocolate sponge. On the bottom layer spread *crème patissière*; on the second, spread half the cream and kiwi fruit. On the third layer, spread sliced strawberries, and on the top and sides spread the remaining cream.

Crêpe Cake

Make 12 crêpes. (See page 57.)

2 tins mandarin oranges
3 tablespoons Cointreau

½ pint / 300 ml double cream,
  whipped

Layer the crêpes in flan tin, sprinkling Cointreau on each one, and putting mandarin oranges between. Cover with tin foil. Heat through in oven at 200°c / 400°F / gas mark 6 for 15 minutes. Cut into slices as you would a cake. Serve hot with cream.

Took Sybil to Holloway Road underground station, on direct line to
Heathrow. What a life she's had! All tumbled out in her last hours
with us. She was married to a man who'd discovered 'the missing
link' between ape and man – the skull of an 8000-year-old woman they
called Mrs Ples. Was it short for 'plesianthropus'? It had made him
famous and he'd been offered a chair at the University of Wisconsin.
Then an operation for something minor, can't remember what, went
wrong and he'd haemorrhaged. Affected his brain. He still func-
tioned but not with the same brilliance. Shortly afterwards one of her
sons was killed in a motor accident. How do people survive such
calamities? If one of my children died it would be the end. Finish me
for good.

Illustration of how I go to pieces: after taking Sybil to the
underground A. and I had a medical examination for insurance. I'd
been dreading it for three days before the event. Said at one point in
the morning I didn't want to go – it's my terror they'll discover
something wrong with me. I'd sooner not know. It's no good telling
me an examination might catch something in time. I can't be rational
about it. I just don't want to know!

Turned out all right. I'm as healthy as sunshine. Just a little
overweight. Can't think why!

Real family lunch today. Della and Ralph; Deana, A.'s second
cousin, and her two children; Aunty Anne who's still with us, she
stayed for a week after coming for the wedding of another second
cousin – too complicated to explain how and on whose side! And my
brood.

Jewish families enjoy cold fried fish, so I offered fat fillets of plaice,
and poached two large trout. Invented a dish: green peppers stuffed
with sweet and sour fish. That's worth passing on. For veg: creamed
potatoes, *haricots verts* and carrots tossed in spring onions fried in
butter and caraway seeds. Simple desserts: fresh fruit salad and apple
strudel with fresh cream.

Ralph looked a little low – still not fully recovered from his by-pass
operation; Deana full of marital trauma. It shouldn't have been a
happy afternoon. But the sun was out and hot. Daniel put up the
badminton net for the kids. After eating and washing up, sat out in
the garden, dodging the bees, enjoying the gorgeous rhododendrons.
Della's son, Adam, came over with his newly wedded wife, Julie, for

tea. Deana borrowed Daniel's guitar, strummed. We all lazed around singing. And to cap the day, I got an unexpected visit from my darling grand-daughter. They'd been to Clacton and turned up expecting to see everyone. But everyone had gone.

Boiled Salmon Trout in Dill Sauce

5 lb / 2.2 kg salmon in cutlets
1 onion, sliced
1 tablespoon fresh dill
1 tablespoon wine vinegar

5 black peppercorns
1 bay leaf
½ pint / 300 ml water
2 teaspoons salt

Boil above ingredients, except the salmon, for 20 minutes in fish kettle. Then add fish cutlets, cover and simmer for 10 minutes. Carefully remove fish with spatula. Place on platter and keep warm.

Dill sauce

2 oz / 50 g butter
2 tablespoons flour
½ pint / 300 ml fish stock
¼ pint / 150 ml single cream

2 egg yolks
1 tablespoon dill
Salt and pepper to taste
Watercress for garnish

Melt butter. Add flour to make roux. Let out with fish stock to make smooth sauce. Stir in cream and egg yolk. Add dill, salt and pepper to taste. Pour over fish. Garnish with watercress.

Green Peppers Stuffed with Sweet and Sour Fish

4 large green peppers
½ lb / 225 g minced raw fish
2 oz / 50 g butter
1 tablespoon chopped onion

1 tablespoon sultanas
Juice of 1 lemon
2 tablespoons single cream

Slice top off peppers. Remove seeds. Put into saucepan. Cover with boiling water to seal skins. Leave for 10 minutes, then drain.

To make filling: melt butter and fry onion for 5 minutes. Add

sultanas, fish and lemon juice. Simmer for 10 minutes. Withdraw from heat. Add single cream. Fill the peppers with this mixture. Place in ovenproof dish, cover and cook for 30 minutes at 200°C / 400°F / gas mark 6.

Apple Strudel

1 lb / 450 g filo pastry	4 oz / 100 g ground almonds
4 large cooking apples, grated	4 oz / 100 g chopped almonds
2 teaspoons cinnamon	1 egg, beaten
8 oz / 225 g sultanas	2 oz / 50 g vanilla sugar
8 oz / 225 g brown sugar	

I buy my filo pastry from a Greek supermarket. It comes in paper-thin sheets. Ensure it's moist and kept moist. It must be pliable for rolling.

Grease a flat baking sheet.

Lay two sheets of the pastry on a teacloth, leaving about 2 in / 5 cm of one end of cloth clear. Mix together fruit, spice and nuts. Spread half over filo sheets, leaving an empty border all round. Lay next two filo sheets over mixture. Spread on remaining mix. Lay another two sheets over. Take clear end of teacloth in both hands, and heave over to form roll. Put two palette knives end to end beneath roll and transfer to flat baking tin. Brush top with beaten egg. Sprinkle over vanilla sugar. Bake at 190°C / 375°F / gas mark 5 for 30 minutes.

Monday 3 June

When you have a house with extra bedrooms, there's a constant flow of people hoping to save hotel bills. On Thursday Yildiz arrives from Turkey. When she rang some months ago to say she was coming she announced that she was going to visit New York for ten days. Her first time there. 'Come with me,' she sprang at me over the phone from Istanbul. It was tempting. The temptation grew. A. pushed me over the edge. We leave on the 10th. It'll be wonderful to share her first experience of a city I love and in which I have so many good friends. Yildiz runs the Istanbul Turko-British Association and is here to interview applicant teachers of English.

So, a busy week ahead – dinner dates, theatre, and the night before I leave for New York I've arranged a dinner party. Must give some thought to that. I've got next Friday and Saturday to do the shopping and what advance preparations I can squeeze in. Not much of

Saturday, though, because we're driving up to Leeds to catch the last night of *Chips With Everything*. A surprise trip for Yildiz. I bet she'll arrive with nuts and real Turkish delight and that dreadfully fattening baklava.

Wednesday
5 June

Alan Bates rang today to apologise that I had to write twice for a reply to my invitation for the 9th and to say he's playing in *Dance Of Death* at the Riverside. They perform on Sundays! The day I especially chose, thinking it would be better for theatre people. Damn! Still, at least *he's* rung. No word from another guest, also an actor. Can't understand why people just don't pick up a phone. I'm not chasing.

Thursday
6 June

Picked up Magda and Natasha to come on a little trip out to Heathrow to meet Yildiz. Everyone should have a friend like 'our mad Turk' who comes from Istanbul heavily laden with pistachio nuts (shelled and unshelled), walnuts, dried apricots, hazelnuts, egg plant, cherries, feta cheese, black olives, their brand of pastrami, and Turkish delight. That's aside from books and blouses and duty-free cigarettes and liquor and postcards from the Topkapi museum. Yildiz promises to make something Turkish for Sunday's party.

Friday
7 June

Am sitting at the kitchen table catching up on notes. Have just made my desserts for Sunday. Needed my cocktail-hour drink, vodka and tonic, and a breather before we go off to a concert at the Barbican. Young Turkish conductor. Yildiz insists we accompany her. One of the pleasures of having guests – though it can misfire as I know to my cost – is that you get caught up in their holiday. It's fine to find myself going to a movie or theatre I might not otherwise have seen; it's hell to have guests who stink one's kitchen out with cigarettes first thing in the morning, or who talk to me while I'm trying to read the post, or who've grabbed the newspaper before I can get to it, or who are full of advice about how I should run the kitchen, my family, my life! Love concerts, though. Don't go to enough of them.

Decided on rum chocolate mousse and summer pudding because this is the time of the year when there's all that fresh fruit about. In fact, I should think about my 50th birthday next year and perhaps make a couple of extra summer puddings to put in the freezer. They say you shouldn't leave things in the freezer for longer than six months. But I'm still alive! Must keep aside enough fruit to make them around August, nine months away from May. Is that too long? Why am I thinking so far ahead? May be dead by then. Must be crazy.

Sat making notes while Yildiz prepared stuffed egg plants. Between note-taking made my duck pâté. Roasted the duck last night, so it was easy to strip the meat from the bones. Boiled the carcass for stock. Those containers of stock in the freezer from past parties always come in handy sooner or later. Tomorrow night, as an alternative to the pâté, I'll use some old stock and make hot, creamy chicken soup because the nights of June 1985 are not as warm as they should be. Last night was 57°. Coldest in eight years. Crazy. It'll be interesting to see who and how many will take soup rather than pâté, though I think – June hot or June cold – people, given a choice, prefer hot starters. *Saturday 8 June*

Wish I had someone to take down my notes while I worked. Yesterday shopping I saw some really fleshy lemon sole fillets. Prefer them fried with a slice of lemon but it'll mean standing in front of the oven and getting my hair all smelly and not being able to sit with my guests. Hate that. Will have to find a way that enables me simply to put them in the oven, forget them, and mingle, pretty and perfumed, with my friends.

Later: Tanya rushing around making her picnic for the Kenwood concerts, a ritual which all the kids enjoy. Gives me great pleasure that they've adopted this classical music event. Just get anxious when the picnic side of it deteriorates into a wild booze-up.

Haven't done as much preparation for tomorrow night as I should. Now have to dash up the M1 to Leeds. We're taking Deborah Holmes, a brilliant young student from the States who's passing her time in London helping Anthony Holden research his biography of Olivier.

Words – the new literary magazine – is planning a special issue on A. and was looking for someone to write 3000 words on his work. He recommended a young student rather than an old hand. Yildiz thinks we're going on a trip up north to have dinner with someone. She's never seen a professional production of one of A.'s plays.

What other woman would be doing this, I ask myself? Got back from Leeds by 1.30 in the morning; had to go for 11 a.m. coffee with someone to collect my first-ever diamond ring which A. had bought *Sunday 9 June*

me as a Christmas present. 'To make up for what I couldn't afford on our wedding day' – it had only just come, though. I've got to cook tonight's dinner party; the house is full of people in different rooms; tomorrow morning Yildiz and I leave for New York – first time off on my own for ages. And I'm not yet packed. And A. is nagging me to make these notes!

Do I enjoy going without 'him'? Unhesitatingly – yes! Why? It's a challenge, that's why. Reassuring. To make my own routines and decisions, to be able to have a holiday of my own rhythms, to know you're not dependent on anyone, that you're being fussed over for your own sake. Previously in New York I've had to meet with people to do with our productions and much as I like theatre people it is, after twenty-seven years, a relief not to have to be facing those competitive egos. Instead I'll be among my friends who are each one of them great cooks. I'll be eating in their homes, in restaurants, going to galleries, looking out for new recipes, having a luuuuverly time. Not that A.'s ever *insisted* I follow *his* rhythms, but partners just do. They restrict each other.

A splendid production of *Chips*. The play still holds up. Full, enthusiastic house. Nick Hytner, the director, had come up to Leeds for the last night. Clever young man. Went backstage to congratulate the cast, full of pretty boys walking around in towels from the shower. They'd given two performances that day. An excellent cast. Not one dud among them. They were very grateful we'd made the effort to journey up. Do you know, there was some hesitation at the box-office as to whether we should or should not pay for the tickets. Fortunately the administrator arrived in time to say 'of course not'. I should think so! Driving all that way up and then have to pay for our own play! *Chips* is on the school syllabus, that's why Leeds Playhouse put it on. I've got fond memories of that theatre. They put on the first UK production of *The Wedding Feast*. John Harrison, the artistic director who also directed the play, came up to apologise for not wearing the woollen jacket I'd knitted for him as a first-night present all those years ago.

Had to have my bath before going to bed despite the late hour, and guess what? Found my grand-daughter in the house. What a welcome-home present! *She's* the one I'm going to miss in New York.

Went to bed at 2 a.m. Couldn't sleep long. Internal alarm woke me up at 6.30.

Must dash soon but a few words about last night's dinner party. All old friends. Roy and Gwen (Shaw) – Sir and Lady now. He's still in the process of adjusting to retirement from being Secretary General of the Arts Council. Not easy. That was a full and demanding life. Suddenly no one needs his favours. You discover your real friends that way. He's writing a book which he was going to call 'People, Art and Politics'. A. told him it was an off-putting title. Paula (Swift) suggested 'The Suffering Muse' which gave Roy the idea of *The Crippled Muse*.

Paula is having a wonderful time. She's back in the acting swim. Just done a film about seven women on a physical hardship course. She's been canoeing, rock climbing, camping. And she's about to become involved in a soap opera called *Albion Market*. Which leaves David at home where he's teaching himself to cook and has started to write. We've known them ever since David played the lead in *The Wedding Feast*. And there were Jack and Denise Gold. Jack's just made a new film from a Jack Rosenthal script called *The Chain*, about seven people involved in moving house. Seems to come in sevens. Odd that Jack and A. have never worked together – they come from similar backgrounds. Denise is also returning to acting. Now that our kids are grown up we suddenly find we can direct our energies in other directions, breathe more freely. It's good.

Everyone pretended to groan and complain because I gave them a choice of starters and main course. Was wrong about people wanting hot starters. It was fifty-fifty, with some tasting both.

Goodbye!

Aubergines Stuffed with Lamb

8 medium aubergines
1 tablespoon vegetable oil
2 lb / 900 g minced lamb
4 small onions, chopped
2 lb / 900 tomatoes, skinned
   and chopped

3 tablespoons chopped parsley
3 tablespoons chopped green
   pepper
Salt and pepper to taste

Bake aubergines whole on baking sheet in oven at 170°C / 325°F / gas mark 3 until soft. Leave to cool for 1 hour.

Heat oil in deep saucepan. Add minced meat. Fry until it changes colour. Add chopped onions. Cook for 15 minutes with lid on. Add tomatoes, parsley, pepper and seasoning. Cook for another 30 minutes without a lid.

Cut cooked aubergines lengthways. Scoop flesh out of each half, mix flesh with meat mixture and fill aubergine shells.

This amount serves 8, but depending upon people's appetite, you may have some left over. It's just as delicious cold.

Duck Pâté

4 lb / 1.8 kg duck
2 medium onions
4 oz / 100 g butter
8 oz / 225 g chicken livers
Grated rind of 1 lemon and
   1 orange

4 tablespoons port
½ teaspoon powdered bay leaf
½ teaspoon rosemary
Salt and pepper to taste

Roast duck, on a rack, for 1½ hours at 200°C / 400°F / gas mark 6.

Fry onions in 1 oz / 25 g of butter. Take all the meat off duck and chop finely together with chicken livers and fried onions. Mix in grated orange and lemon rind, port, bay leaf, rosemary, salt and pepper.

Pour into terrine. Melt remaining butter and pour over. Cover with lid. Bake in pan of water for 45 minutes at 190°C / 375°F / gas mark 5.

Creamy Chicken Soup

4 lb / 1.8 kg boiling chicken
2 sticks celery, chopped
1 large onion, chopped
1 bouquet garni
Salt and pepper to taste

2 oz / 50 g butter
2 oz / 50 g flour
2 egg yolks
½ pint / 300 ml double cream

Put chicken in large saucepan with vegetables, bouquet garni, salt and pepper. Boil for 2 hours until tender. Remove from saucepan. Strain liquid. Leave to cool so that you can skim off excess fat. Keep mushy vegetables.

Melt butter. Add flour to make roux. Let out with 1 pint / 600 ml of chicken stock. Reheat for 10 minutes or just short of boiling. Remove from heat. Stir in egg yolks, cream and mushy vegetables. Serve immediately.

Remove flesh from chicken and freeze for future use.

8 fat fillets of sole

1 large onion, chopped

½ pint / 300 ml of white wine

2 small bay leaves

Salt and pepper to taste

Grease 12 in / 30 cm dish well.

Lay chopped onions on base. Roll fillets and lay them side by side. Pour over white wine. Add bay leaves, salt and pepper. Cook for 20 minutes at 200°C / 400°F / gas mark 6. Strain liquid for sauce but keep fish hot.

Cream sauce

½ pint / 300 ml fish stock

1 oz / 25 g butter

1 oz / 25 g flour

¼ pint / 150 ml single cream

1 tablespoon lemon juice

Melt butter. Add flour to make roux. Let out with fish liquid. Stir in cream and lemon juice. Pour over fish. Put back in oven at 170°C / 325°F / gas mark 3 to reheat for 15 minutes.

Summer Pudding

8 large slices white bread, crusts
  removed

4 oz / 100 g sugar

2 tablespoons water

½ lb / 225 g raspberries

½ lb / 225 g redcurrants

½ lb / 225 g blackcurrants

½ lb / 225 g strawberries

1 pint / 600 ml double cream,
  whipped

Grease 1½ lb / 700 g pudding basin.

Cook fruit in saucepan with sugar and water for 5 minutes until it begins to look a little mushy. Line basin on the bottom and sides with 5 slices of bread. Overlap bread so that it holds together when turned out. Pile in fruit with juice. Lay 3 slices of bread on top. Place a tea plate on the top with a heavy weight, to press contents down overnight. (I use an old flat iron.) Turn out on to a plate next day and serve with whipped cream.

I always try to keep two summer puddings in my freezer for special occasions.

Rum Chocolate Mousse

6 oz / 175 g plain chocolate
3 tablespoons Jamaica rum
2 eggs, separated
¼ teaspoon vanilla

3 oz / 75 g castor sugar
½ pint / 300 ml double cream, whipped

Melt chocolate with rum in a double boiler. Blend in the 2 egg yolks and vanilla. Leave to cool. Whisk egg whites until stiff. Fold in sugar. Whisk cream until thick. Blend chocolate mix into cream. Fold in egg whites. Pour into small ramekins. Chill in fridge.

Thursday 20 June Literally crawled into the house this morning after a very pleasant flight from New York on British Airways. Not being able to sleep on the plane completely exhausted me. Not sure I'll be able to finish this entry. Travelled with 'The Third World' pop group. Fascinating. Expected at any moment a wild party would start at the back of the plane. Couldn't believe that musicians would be able to sit still for seven hours, or not to want to use the time rehearsing. Naïve really. Nothing happened. Everybody slept. Except me.

A. met us, of course. Hoped he'd bring Natasha. Told me he'd thought about it but didn't feel he could ask Magda to wake the baby so early. As he walked away from us in the car park to get the car, I called out: 'I expected you to turn up with the new car.' He called back: 'You know we can't afford a new car, what made you even imagine I'd do such a thing?' He disappeared up to the 4th floor and left us waiting with the luggage. No car appeared. But he did, rushing downstairs to us to say there was no way to our level. I *knew* there was and told him so – who should know if not me, I've had to drive so

many visitors to their planes – but it seemed easier to get in the lift with the luggage and get to his level. Only he'd forgotten to say which *was* his level! He's not always with it, my old man. We finally met up. And there was the new car. Just the kind of thing he enjoys doing, springing surprises. Don't we all! 'What about the overdraft?' I asked. 'What overdraft?' replied my impetuous husband.

God knows how he keeps his cool about an overdraft. Suppose because we've lived on one for so long. The problem for playwrights is that they never know when money is coming in from where and for how much. Somehow it keeps coming, in lots of small amounts from different ends of the world. I may thank God for the foreigners but one day we'll have to sell the house. I put the idea to him every so often which at once sends him into depression. Dare I ever bring it up again?

Arrived at Bishops Road in a bleary state to find the second surprise: Natasha waiting for me. A. had arranged it with Magda. Tanya there too. Lovely to be greeted by a family. Had eggs and bacon. A. suggested champagne but I couldn't face it. We'd had some on the plane besides. Staggered around not really wanting to give in to sleep because I thought if I do I'll never be able to sleep the night. A. had arranged to take Tanya, Yildiz and me to the House of Commons to hear the Rabbi Julia Neuberger lecture on the regression of women's rights in the 80s. Not for me. Wasn't up to it, even though I'd collapsed briefly at 4 p.m. for an hour.

Sent Tanya out to buy chicken. Will make dinner for us all before they leave. Nothing special, just pieces thrown into my orange Le Creuset pot with vegetables. Have to do it. I'm somebody who cooks a supper every night, even if only for A. and me.

Checked diary to see what lay ahead. Straight back into entertaining. On Sunday I have two, maybe four people for lunch, and in the evening one or maybe three for dinner. And there's a houseful of people to feed – family, children, friends. So tomorrow, Friday, have to get my skates on and do the shopping.

Tanya returned high from the Neuberger lecture which was about how women had lost many of the gains they'd imagined they'd secured in the 60s. Could turn out to be a momentous event for her. She's declared quite definitely that she wants to return to study and that she now knew what she wanted to take her BA in: Women's Studies.

Managed to keep awake till now. It's 10.30. But I'm fading . . .

Friday	Within short space of time, hours, it had seemed as though I'd never
21 June	been away. Got up early and went off to shop. Bought lamb chops,

Friday
21 June
Within short space of time, hours, it had seemed as though I'd never been away. Got up early and went off to shop. Bought lamb chops, some lovely lean beef, poussin and – now what was the last thing I bought? God! It escapes me. I *did* buy one other thing . . . Oh yes! spare ribs. *There's* a selection of things to carry us over the weekend, I thought.

Must rush to get ready for the Savile Club.

Saturday
22 June
Returned not only to feeding but to being fed!

Yesterday, the evening after my return from New York, went to the Savile Club. Host: Richard Adams, of *Watership Down* fame. Hates being known only for his first work. A. also complains about what he calls 'the frozen image'. Applies to most artists, I suppose. Richard was having a Mid-Summer's Day dinner party. He invited us; John Braine and his lady friend; Francis King – theatre critic and novelist; the crime writer – Ruth Rendell; and a teacher of drama from Bristol who sat with her right leg stretched out in a splint.

Prawn cocktails for starters. Instead of shredded lettuce on the base there was chopped-up watercress. Unusual, that. Followed by half a duck each, small, but a whole half with blackcurrant sauce. Now I'd never had that. Duck with cherry, duck with orange, but never this combination of tartiness with well-cooked, moist duck meat. Very successful. Perhaps one could serve duck with any fruit – pineapple, apricot? Determined to recreate it. Liked Richard Adams. Courteous, old-fashioned gent.

Today had a run-around evening fulfilling two dates which we'd accidentally double-booked. The first was to have been with Mira Coopman to watch on Channel 4 a documentary film she'd secretly made in South Africa called 'Maids & Madams'. But we'd also agreed to go to Margaret Windham's 30th birthday. She's A.'s radio producer. Did *Caritas*, *Yardsale* and recently *Bluey*, the play she'd urged him to write specially for the European Radio Commission 1984. We went to eat with Mira promising we'd video the film to view at home. She fed us radishes, celery and houmous dips. Margaret gave us lasagne. Two full houses. Made me dizzy.

Here's what I baked for dessert. The only complete recipe I came home with from New York was one for a prune and pecan cake. Didn't have any pecans but had walnuts. Didn't have any buttermilk but had sour cream. Followed the recipe with everything but the pecans and buttermilk, which is what I mean when I say I never follow a recipe! Improvisation! Use what you have. It baked beautifully, looked very good, but can't be tasted until the Sunday lunch party. Have to be patient.

A dessert I enjoyed in a New York Cuban restaurant was mango cream pie. Hadn't tasted that before. Couldn't find an exact recipe for it, but found something similar which I experimented upon to make it come out as I remember having tasted it. The recipe called for gelatine dissolved in four tablespoonfuls of water, and it also included four tablespoonfuls of lime juice. Now, having made it, I think the gelatine should be dissolved in the lime juice and the water dispensed with, because the two together created too much liquid. Kept it in the fridge overnight but it still hadn't set sufficiently. Wasn't as firm as it should have been. It should have cut into nice even slices. Otherwise a good dessert. Small pieces of mango set in the creamy substance, a fresh taste. Strongly recommend it with graham crackers as the base. I'd returned with a small supply of them which I prefer to use, rather than digestive biscuits, for cheesecake. They make a finer crumb.

New York seems a long way away. Can't believe I was there only two days ago. Yildiz here for another two weeks. Want to show her as much as we can, to give her what an American friend called 'dining out' stories. 'I want you,' said this friend who's coming for three days in August, 'to make a dinner with interesting people, because I need stories I can dine out on.' Fond of him though I am, told him I didn't like his attitude. Distressing to think people need other people's lives to enliven their evenings out. We're planning trips to Stratford to see *The Merry Wives Of Windsor* – Sheila's playing Mistress Quickly – and a weekend in Norfolk for a barn-roof raising.

Don't know why I slept till 10.30 this morning. Woke with a start. *Sunday* Seven of us for lunch, including the kids and Joan and Dannie Abse. *23 June* Two of the warmest, most unpretentious people I know. Love the way they involve everyone in a conversation, the youngsters as well as the adults. Dannie's gentle manner must be due to the combination of doctor and poet. They'd been on one of Yildiz's lecture and reading jaunts in Turkey.

Wasn't much to do. Had the poussins I bought on Friday halved so that everybody would get a leg and a little breast. Fried them in onions and a mixture of butter and oil, salt, pepper and garlic, turning them to make sure they were brown on both sides. Placed them in the oven which both kept them hot and finished them off. Chicken pieces never cook through by merely frying. Turned out good. Had a special taste. Everyone commented on it and, though it happened quite by accident, it's worth recording.

Enjoyed having the man at my table whose voice often comes to me in my kitchen. Often, as I cook, I listen to Dannie introducing poetry requests. Joan announced that her book listing the contents of every art gallery in the land had been published at last. What a work!

And then – oh yes – had to cut the grass. No one had cut it while I was in the States. Persuaded Daniel to cut and I raked it, so we were able to make the garden look a little tidier before the rains came. Had to have a shower before I could think about what I'd make for Ronnie Lee who was coming for dinner. Couldn't face another meal of meat. Decided to use up some smoked trout. Took it off the bone, sliced the flesh and mixed it together with two sliced avocados, sliced spring onions, all on a bed of cos lettuce. Sprinkled mock caviar over the top and added French dressing. Followed with tortelline – a pasta without too much meat. Made a *pesto* sauce. But this called for a whole cup of olive oil. Couldn't use that amount. Only used half. Compensated by adding a carton of single cream to help let it out. Also chopped up and added some mozzarella cheese which further helped to give it a creamy consistency. So it's *pesto* with a difference, although my New York friend still recognised it.

Started off with champagne. Ronnie had one portion of the pasta dish, though he kept up a random pronging of his fork into the main bowl, a habit I hate. Am so fond of him that I basked in his pleasure more than I suffered from this unbearable trait. He probably had two helpings by the time he'd finished pronging, even three! Which cook can resist such appreciation?

Then he started on the salad. Had five helpings of that! For dessert I offered baked bananas and ginger in Cointreau and cream. Also served him walnut and prune cake with whipped cream. Giggle as I write this, because it's everything a New York Jew on guard against a high cholesterol intake should not take in! But I have this soft spot for Ronnie and wanted to make a special fuss of him. What didn't help his self-control was the arrival of Natasha. Ronnie is dotty about children – has three daughters and two adopted sons. He had to perform for my grand-daughter. He set up a routine which involved him doing the rounds of the desserts again and again and flinging them into his dish and screaming in a way that brought forth squeals of delight from my little girl. The second bottle of champagne couldn't have helped either. Ronnie is over here setting up a production of a musical version of *Charley's Aunt*. The theatre is no guarantee of champagne, double cream or even bread and butter. Let him eat and be happy while it lasts!

Prune and Pecan Cake

4 oz / 100 g butter
9 oz / 250 g sugar
2 eggs
½ pint / 300 ml buttermilk
4 oz / 100 g sifted flour
½ teaspoon salt

½ teaspoon baking powder
1½ teaspoons nutmeg
8 oz / 225 g prunes, chopped
Rind and juice of 1 lemon
8 oz / 225 g pecan nuts, chopped

Grease 8 in / 20 cm cake tin.

Cream butter with sugar. Beat in eggs and buttermilk. Fold in the flour, sifted with salt, baking powder and nutmeg. Fold in prunes, lemon juice and pecans. Bake at 190°C / 375°F / gas mark 5 for 40 minutes or until knife comes out clean. Walnuts and sour cream can be used instead of pecans and buttermilk.

Mango Cream Pie

8 oz / 225 g shortcrust pastry
1 oz / 25 g gelatine
3 tablespoons lime juice

1½ lb / 675 g mango flesh
4 oz / 100 g sugar
½ pint / 300 ml double cream

Grease 10 in / 25 cm flan tin.

Bake shortcrust pastry blind for 20 minutes at 200°C / 400°F / gas mark 6. Melt gelatine in lime juice. Mix mango, sugar and double cream. Combine two mixtures. Pour into pastry case to set.

Instead of pastry I prefer to use crumbs of graham crackers, but these are American and not always available in the U K. The nearest to them is something called Biscuit Crumb. If you find either, mix 8 oz / 225 g with 2 tablespoons of melted butter and press this around a flan tin to form a crust. No need to bake.

Tortelline and Pesto Sauce (with a difference)

2 lb / 900 g tortelline
2 oz / 50 g fresh basil, finely
    chopped
4 cloves garlic, crushed
¼ pint / 150 ml olive oil

¼ pint / 150 ml single cream
1 oz / 25 g mozzarella cheese
Salt and freshly ground black
    pepper to taste

Simply blend above ingredients – except tortelline, of course – to make *pesto*. Cook tortelline and serve with sauce.

Bananas with Cointreau

1 oz / 25 g butter
6 large bananas
3 tablespoons brown sugar
Juice from 1 lemon

3 tablespoons water
2–3 tablespoons Cointreau
Stem ginger

Butter shallow ovenproof dish. Peel and cut the bananas lengthways. Lay in dish. Sprinkle sugar over top. Add the lemon juice and water. Bake at 190°C / 375°F / gas mark 5 for 20 minutes. Add the Cointreau just before the end. Scatter small pieces of stem ginger on top.

You can use rum or Grand Marnier. Crème de Menthe might be interesting.

Monday
24 June

Slept again until 10.30. Obviously haven't yet got over jet lag. Had a pile of ironing to catch up with. General tidying up after the weekend. A. announced that Julian Alexander and his friend, Adolfo, from Paris would arrive around tea-time and stay for supper. All go to the Mermaid in the evening. Julian's the son of Susana Alexander who translated, produced, directed and acted in *The Four Seasons* in Mexico City. A. said it was the best production of that difficult play he'd ever seen. Came back

full of ideas for trimming and re-shaping it. Hopes for an opportunity to direct the new version. Keeps turning down requests for its performance here and in New York. Wants the right set-up. How do you find the 'right' set- up? Julian's studying at the Sorbonne.

Asked A. how he intended getting six people in the car – Tanya and Yildiz were coming too. 'We'll manage somehow,' he replied, as he always does. Did he want to eat out or was I to cook something? A meal out for six would be costly. I'd cook something. Went to buy chicken for frying. Fried nine portions. Enough for us and some left over for Daniel who, I knew, would come in later. Made saffron rice with mushrooms and onions. Big salad of three coloured peppers with chopped celery and spring onions. Wanted the remains of the mango cream pie finished. It was!

Just returned from the theatre having dropped the boys off at Camden Town. Saw *Breaking The Silence* by Stephen Poliakoff. Understand from A.'s agent Nat the play suffered moving from The Pit to a larger theatre.

Another very very hectic day. Said to Tanya: 'Where's the time for leisure? There's no more time for leisure. It's one errand after another to do with the house. Shopping, cooking, ironing . . . no let-up.' On the other hand it's all relative, isn't it? Some women would view my life as rich, varied and eventful. And, no doubt, given leisure I'd fill it with more of the same.

Chicken in Saffron Rice

3 lb / 1.3 kg chicken	2 courgettes
2 tablespoons flour	3 large tomatoes, skinned
Salt and pepper to taste	and chopped
3 tablespoons vegetable oil	2 green peppers, chopped
2 medium onions, chopped	½ pint / 300 ml white wine

Joint the chicken. Mix flour, salt and pepper. Roll chicken pieces in seasoned flour, then fry in oil until brown. Remove from pan. Add vegetables to the oil. Fry for a few minutes. Place vegetables at base of an ovenproof casserole. Lay chicken pieces on top. Add wine. Cover and cook for 1 hour at 190°C / 375°F / gas mark 5.

Saffron rice

1 lb / 450 g long grain rice	Generous pinch saffron
1 large onion, chopped	4 oz / 100 g sultanas, pre-washed
1 tablespoon vegetable oil	4 oz / 100 g pine nuts
1 pint / 600 ml chicken stock, fresh if possible	Salt and pepper to taste

Using a large saucepan, fry chopped onion in oil until brown. Add rice. Cook and stir for 10 minutes on low heat. Add chicken stock and saffron. Cover with lid and allow to simmer gently for 25 minutes, when rice should have absorbed all liquid. Add sultanas and nuts and salt and pepper to taste.

Place chicken pieces in centre of large platter. Spoon rice around the edge.

Tuesday 2 July Took Yildiz to Stratford on Friday to see Sheila play Mistress Quickly. Last night to the King's Head to hear Stephan Bednarchuck in cabaret. In between, had a nostalgic trip back to Norfolk for a barn-roof raising.

Yildiz and I loved *Merry Wives*. A. hated it. Sheila made us a very rich and tasty lasagne in her flat where we partied with her mother and Peter Jeffries who played Falstaff. Must get the recipe from her. The King's Head evening was a sparse affair. Always enjoy the atmosphere but not the food. Bednarchuck is that kind of highly talented performer who, so far, has not found a specially individual style.

If A.'s sister Della and her husband Ralph hadn't moved from London to Norfolk in the early 50s to live a simple, rural life making furniture by hand and rearing chickens, I wouldn't have met A. and I don't suppose I'd be here writing this book. A. lived and worked with Ralph for a while, and one of the (criminal, they now consider it) acts they committed was to pull down an old barn. More than thirty years later, the cottage is their country retreat and Ralph is rebuilding the barn. Last weekend their family, friends, Yildiz, A. and I joined them to help hoist the trusses for the barn roof. One of those glorious family get-togethers with a lot of eating and chatter. We were thirteen round the table each time Della had to feed us. I cooked an apple flan and some brownies for the weekend. Collected my mother to join us for the day on Sunday.

The house is called Hill House, one full of special memories for me. I'd never encountered a Jewish family before and, although I was a lively, outgoing personality myself, this lot seemed very strange. My mother had asked me all those years ago why I'd brought a gypsy into the house! God knows what Della thought her younger brother had brought along! All I know is their floorboards creaked as I made my way in the middle of the night to his room; though why – now I come to write about it – it should have been me and not him who creaked from room to room for naughty nights, I can't imagine. Don't want to paint days rosy that weren't, but I think they were, and I miss them.

Can't sit here scribbling much longer. Must bake something special for Ineko Arima who's coming for tea this afternoon. She's the Japanese actress who's to play Annie Wobbler in Tokyo in August. We met her in Japan a couple of years ago when she sat by us in a train carrying actors and playwrights to an audience-gathering in the mountains. Through an interpreter she said how much she would like to perform one of our plays. Well, it's happening. She's a glamorous star out there and Annie will be a very different challenge for her. We hear she's full of nerves about it, which is one of the reasons she's coming to talk with the author. She travels with a young actress who carries her bags, and no doubt she'll bring an interpreter from the Japanese Embassy, someone who knows nothing about theatre and so the language will be doubly difficult for him to interpret!

Think I'll bake them a honey and hazelnut cake to have with ice cream.

Apple Flan

1 lb / 450 g shortcrust pastry

Line a 10 in / 25 cm tart tin with pastry and bake blind for 20 minutes at 190°C / 375°F / gas mark 5.

Crème pâtissière

4 oz / 175 g sugar	5 egg yolks, beaten
2 tablespoons cornflour	Several drops vanilla
¾ pint / 400 ml milk	1 dessertspoon kirsch

Combine sugar and cornflour. Add to milk. Bring to boil, stirring constantly. Blend milk mixture into beaten egg yolks. Add vanilla and kirsch. Leave to cool.

Filling

1½ lb / 675 g cooking apples, peeled and thinly sliced	1 oz / 25 g butter 2 oz / 50 g sugar

Arrange apple slices on buttered baking tin. Dot with knobs of butter. Dust with sugar. Grill under low flame until golden brown. Don't forget to turn them.

By now cream should be cool. Spread it on base of pastry case. Lay slices of apple in decorative pattern over cream.

Apricot glaze

6 tablespoons apricot jam 3 tablespoons water	1 tablespoon kirsch

Warm apricot jam with water, stirring until mixture is smooth. Add kirsch. Brush top of apple slices with this glaze.

Put back into oven for another 15 minutes at 190°C / 375°F / gas mark 5.

Brownies

7 oz / 200 g bitter sweet chocolate	8 oz / 225 g sugar 1 teaspoon vanilla
5 oz / 150 g butter	4 oz / 100 g flour
4 eggs	5 oz / 150 g chopped walnuts
¼ teaspoon salt	

Grease shallow baking sheet.

Using a double boiler, melt chocolate with butter. Take off heat. Beat egg and salt. Beat in sugar and vanilla. Transfer warm chocolate into a mixing bowl. Stir in egg mixture. Fold in flour and nuts. Pour into baking tray. Bake at 190°C / 375°F / gas mark 5 for 35 minutes. When cool, cut into small squares.

2 oz / 50 g ground hazelnuts	5 eggs, separated
2 tablespoons sugar	4 oz / 100 g clear honey
2½ oz / 65 g self-raising flour, sifted	4 tablespoons double cream

Grease 8 in / 20 cm cake tin.

Mix hazelnuts, sugar and flour. Blend yolks, honey and cream. Fold in the flour mixture. Beat egg whites until stiff. Fold into cake mixture.

Bake at 150°c / 300°F / gas mark 2 for 30 minutes.

Sunday night. Decided to light the barbecue at about 7.30. Assumed *Sunday* everyone, having been invited for 7.30, would arrive, at the latest, by *7 July* 8 p.m. in time for dinner. Everyone did arrive at 8, including my dear friend Nikki Gavron who always experiences difficulty disengaging herself from the last appointment to make it in time for the next one. Everyone except Adrienne Corrie, who arrived very late, which rather spoilt the taste of the lamb.

The barbecuing had been carefully timed. Spread rosemary over the charcoal hoping the meat would pick up the flavour. Tanya and I deliberately undercooked the lamb because Jeremy King, one of the guests and *restaurateur exceptionale* of the Caprice had, on walking through the door and seeing what I was doing, expressed a wish that his meat be almost raw. We gauged the extra amount of cooking that would take place while keeping it warm in the oven, but all our calculations went to pot.

Adrienne rang at around 8 saying she was running late and would be there in fifteen minutes from St John's Wood. At 8.15 no Adrienne. I apologised to the other guests. None of them seemed worried, they were all enjoying one another in the garden. 8.15 became 8.30 became 8.45 became 9. I said to A. this was ridiculous. He said Adrienne would understand if we went ahead and began feeding people.

Who was there? William and Clare Frankel who hadn't been able to make it the other night. Jeremy and Debra and Debra's parents, Sam-the-surgeon and his bubbly wife called Bubbles, whom we'd entertained once before and who'd said they wanted to see us again. Richard Appignanesi, one of our oldest friends, full of black wit and gloom because of the crass reception of his first novel.

Started off with a very successful salmon terrine, in a white wine sauce which gave it a tangy taste. I'd marinated the salmon in sherry and combined it with cod and whiting. Looked and tasted as I intended: a light fish starter. At the end of which Adrienne burst in upon us, hot with apologies and explanations about having been misdirected by idiots she'd stopped in the street. She was mortified and needed a glass of white wine, red wine, anything! Straight away! She's a good talker at the calmest of times, now under pressure of embarrassment she turned full blast upon the gentle, unsuspecting surgeon who sat confused and helpless before her torrent of autobiography. I like Adrienne. She's a good soul. No bullshit. I admire the energy and intelligence she has channelled into things outside her acting career. Gives us all hope. But she does overstimulate one. And by the time Sam took his coffee he looked as though he'd been in the ring for ten rounds.

I know that the pleasure of a real barbecue consists in everyone being around while the meats are cooking, so they can watch and smell it and eat it immediately off the grill; a primitive instinct is satisfied, memories of good old barbaric times stirred. But because I have this need not to be working when my guests have arrived, I want to drink and relax with them, so I aim to get as much done ahead as I can. Consequently I barbecued the meats and then put them in the oven, hoping they wouldn't have to stay there for too long. The lamb turned out as I feared – somewhat overcooked. It had a good flavour nevertheless, and an onion sauce compensated for loss of moisture. Guests reassured me the meat was tender enough, but it wasn't as I would have liked it to be. On the other hand, it's not every night we have the pleasure of Adrienne for dinner!

No sooner had I started serving the lamb than Magda blew in, with Natasha, who of course had to be handed around. Drew up a chair at the already overcrowded table and shared my dinner with her. I'd made sweet and sour red cabbage and had boiled the new potatoes, but I'd wanted the *haricots verts* to be crisp so I had them cooking while we ate starters.

If I can look at my table and see everyone engaged in conversation, I know all's going well. They were. I was satisfied. Richard was deep into life and literature with Yildiz and Clare. Nikki was discovering Jeremy had been a merchant banker, something new to me. William and Bubbles were hitting it off. And I'd deliberately placed Debra next to A. because she once worked with him on the International Playwrights Committee of which he'd been chairman. I guessed they'd have a lot to catch up on, especially as Debra had just started working for Tariq Ali's newly formed film company, Bandung Productions. Sam was listening to Adrienne.

I take a lot of care when I place people at my table. It's important.

Desserts being my favourites, I was my usual abundant self. Made three. Little individual fruit tarts of black and white grapes, cherries and strawberries which are in season, so one wants to use them as much as possible. To the fruit remaining from the tarts I added fresh apricots, chopped pineapples and a little kirsch to make a huge fruit salad. Third was the 'Five-Thousand-Years-of-Suffering Cheese-cake'! Story as follows: Professor Bob Skloot, head of drama at Madison University, Wisconsin, had once been a judge of cheesecake competitions. One day he came to lunch and I offered him two different cheesecakes to sample. He made his choice but next day I received an alternative recipe in the post. And that's what he called it. 'Five-Thousand-Years-of-Suffering Cheesecake'. The great thing about my original recipe (on page 21) is that you can play all sorts of variations upon it. You can flavour the mixture lemon or vanilla, you can alter the texture with nuts or sultanas . . . the possibilities are endless. Not sure about this one. Try it!

When I was first asked to write a cook book, I was very flattered. Then I became anxious. Cooking depends upon so many variables. And, as I've gone deeper into this book, I've become even more anxious. Once I felt like giving up. I find it very hard to write out precise recipes. It's not simply that I don't always measure my quantities; I sometimes deliberately alter them. It depends on my moods. A recipe might call for 2 oz of butter but I may feel in the mood to make the dish richer by putting in 3 oz. Or I may be feeling virtuous and only want to use 1 oz. I may want my pastry to be hard or I may want it to be absorbent. I may want my meat dish to be meaty or I may want it to be impregnated with a marinade. I can't emphasise enough that cooking has not so much to do with good recipes as it has to do with a combination of experience, individual taste, spontaneous imagina-tion, mood, inventiveness and the guests for whom you're cooking. It's an imprecise skill and it worries me to be getting together a book that makes it seem as though I'm saying: 'Follow me and you'll have a good meal.' There! That's got that off my chest. Back to my dinner.

On the whole, the evening went very well. Served coffee in the lounge – A. insisted. Still not convinced it doesn't disrupt good conversation around the dinner table. Of course some guests may be grateful for the change, but others are happy to remain with the partners they find themselves next to. We're both right. I remember a party where, came the dessert, the men had to move to the left of the woman on their left. Not a bad ritual, I suppose.

In the lounge two groups at once took shape. Nikki, Richard and Adrienne, each of them a visual arts authority, got into heated discussion. Not sure what the heat was over, just heard the name Hogarth raised again and again. The rest of us gathered at the fireplace end of the room. No fights there! Richard and Adrienne were the last to leave. A. got on to his familiar complaint about not having gone to university and wanting to give up writing in order to return to study. Richard had heard it all before. Adrienne told him to stop talking about it and do it.

A. drove Richard home. By the time he returned Natasha was awake and we all had a rollick on the bed with her. Asleep by 2.30 a.m.

Five-Thousand-Years-Of-Suffering Cheesecake

5 oz / 125 g graham cracker or digestive biscuit crumbs	3 tablespoons flour
	Grated rind 1 lemon
2 oz / 50 g melted butter	Grated rind ½ orange
1 oz / 25 g sugar	5 eggs
2½ lb / 1.1 kg cream cheese	2 egg yolks
7 oz / 200 g sugar	2 tablespoons double cream

Mix butter, sugar and graham crackers to make crust.

Butter inside of 10 in / 25 cm loose-bottomed tin. Press crust into bottom and sides.

Beat cream cheese until fluffy. Add sugar, flour, lemon and orange rind and eggs, one at a time. Beat well. Add extra yolks. Stir in cream. Pour into tin. Bake at 220°c / 425°F / gas mark 7 for 10 minutes, and then at 170°c / 325°F / gas mark 3 for exactly one hour (even if it looks less brown on top than it should).

Cool. Discard rest of meal and all dirty dishes, mumble prayer to St Caloria, and devour while uttering obscene noises.

Yildiz left by minicab for Heathrow at 6.30 a.m. Had a rough sleepless night. Overslept the time we'd agreed to wake and say goodbye. At 10.30 Carol arrived from Hampshire, Massachusetts, our new house guest. I'd been shopping for tomorrow's dinner party. Decided on duck. Am so passionate about duck I want to cook it as many different ways as possible. This weekend decided to cook it with blackcurrant sauce, just as I'd had it with Richard Adams at the Savile Club.

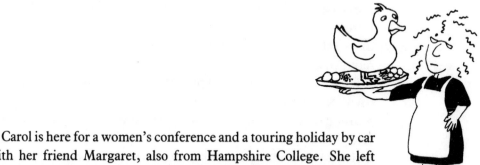

Carol is here for a women's conference and a touring holiday by car with her friend Margaret, also from Hampshire College. She left immediately for Conway Hall. Agreed that, if weather held, we'd go to open air concert in Kenwood. Weather did hold until Brahms 4th Symphony after the interval. We'd enjoyed ourselves until then. I'd whipped up a spinach quiche which was still hot as we picnicked among the crowds waiting for concert to begin. Also concocted a mixed salad. A. buttered bagels which we ate with cheese and grapes and washed down with red wine. For dessert finished off box of chocolate truffles someone had bought me from Fortnum and Mason's. God, they were good! Kenwood is becoming north London's Glyndebourne. Difference is that, though the crowds take great pains over their picnic fare, the musical fare costs much less. Great event. My kids took out season tickets this year. The only reason they weren't using them today is because they were recording on tape the mammoth Live Aid concert which the world, apart from us, seemed to be watching. Carol accompanied by lovely friend/ colleague, Jill, who teaches at Sussex and sometimes at Hampshire.

Returned from concert. Dried out. Offered Jill one of my loose leisure gowns. Instead she emerged in one of Carol's nightgowns. It had frills. Amused Jill. 'Makes me feel all different,' she bubbled on. 'Clothes do maketh the woman, it seems!' A confession from a hardened feminist. She and Carol decided to get Tanya round kitchen table to talk about her future. Men excluded. A. dismissed to lounge to read. They advised her about her new plans to return to study. Even got her excited about the idea of studying in Hampshire. Helpful sisters!

Monday
15 July
Again had little sleep on Saturday night. Friday night had been disrupted worrying about Yildiz's flight. Saturday night baby-sat over Natasha while L.J. and Magda went to a gig. He works hard, my eldest son, always rushing off to concerts or discos in search of that one group that will make the top ten and bring him fame and fortune. I worry when he's driving back through the night tired from Bradford or Leicester or somewhere in deepest Devon. They returned around 12.30 and took their patient babe home.

I'd got up early hoping to prepare things for that night's dinner party. No such luck. At 11.45 A. was nagging me to get ready for the drinks date in Knightsbridge with his old Harper and Row editor, Joan Khan. Joan now works for St Martin's Press in New York. Insisted I send the first sheets of this book to her. Could have a co-production on our hands. If I ever finish it!

Her party included her sister; a young woman over here to write a profile of Mike Frayn for *The New Yorker*; and a distributor of theatre books who said he'd once met us in Joan's flat. Gentle, Jewish man. Very understanding about us not remembering. The nightmare of our life: constantly meeting people I've fed who remember each dish I served them. I can remember neither them nor the dishes. One way of judging people is by the degree of offence they take because we do not recollect them. Those with imagination understand.

Crazily, I'd also accepted an invitation from Nikki to share a barbecue lunch with her kids and friends. On we rushed to the next date. The Gavron boys, Cy and Gerra, were home together. A rare coincidence. We've known them for about 23 years. Good to have watched them grow and find careers. Cy runs Carcanet Press in New York. Gerra is on *The Economist*. Handsome boys. And Nikki's own daughters, Jessica and Sara, tall and stunning. Gives me great pleasure.

Nikki, late with everything as usual, had only just started grilling her marinated chicken and sausages. Found myself eating lunch at 3.30 with a dinner staring me in the face only four hours away and which I had yet to cook. Couldn't stay long. Pity! There were old friends I'd like to have gossiped with. And Helen Suzman, campaigner for sanity and black civil rights in South Africa, she was a guest. Had to miss her. Bad organisation!

Back to Bishops Road kitchen. Pushed A. into action slicing courgettes and carrots, and topping and tailing the *haricots verts*. Carol had scraped the potatoes in the morning. Cut flabby skin from off the duck; melted down the fat with onions to use for roast potatoes at a future date.

Into the middle of all this arrived John Crow, administrator from the Phoenix Theatre in Leicester, delivering my plastic containers in which I'd transported food for the first night. Gave him coffee from a big pot I'd just made, chatted about theatre affairs, but had to carry on cooking. When he was ready to leave, Lisa, John and Joshua dropped in to say hello. Hard to concentrate but, being my well-organised self, I'd laid table the day before, duck was on its way, and the hors d'oeuvre I'd planned was simple to prepare – melon and parma ham. Still, packed them off into the lounge and was able to get myself together in time to join them for a brief exchange before putting on my skates to get ready for 7.30 guests who didn't, in fact, arrive until 8.

Gave my poor guests problem of choosing between a dessert of summer pudding and banana flambé. Not that they ever do choose. Usually they have both. Seems as though dessert is something people deny themselves at home and make pigs of themselves 'abroad'. A. criticises me for putting both desserts on plate at same time. 'You should give them the pleasure of savouring the different tastes one at a time.' Maybe! But when I ask people what they want they say 'both' in such a way that I feel they're like kids who want it *all*. Now! In case, by the time they're ready for the second one, it's gone!

A good evening. The three husbands were business men involved in arts and entertainment. Nathan Joseph, A.'s agent, had once created his own record company; Brian Shepherd was managing director of A & M, the record company for which Lindsay Joe had just started work; Neville Shulman, accountant and artists' manager. He's a man with restless energy, wide interests and a modest, unassuming demeanour. A. had asked him to take on chairmanship of the International Theatre Institute. He'd agreed.

Always fascinates me how lives cross. One: as a young man Neville had been a lighting technician of events taking place at Centre 42, the arts centre A. tried to create in the Roundhouse at

Chalk Farm. A. had forgotten! Neville understood. Two: Brian's wife, Janene, had recently acted in *One More Ride On The Merry-Go-Round* in Leicester. Brian, when he'd just taken over as managing director of A & M Records, and long before we auditioned Janene, had Lindsay Joe on his list of new bloods he planned to attract into the company. Three: Nathan's mother, when she knew her son was taking on A. as a client two years ago, unearthed a letter Nathan had written to her when he was a student at Oxford in which he'd raved about a play he'd just seen by a playwright he prophesied would be one of the greats of the future. The play was *Roots*! And now he was managing that playwright!

Have a lot in common with his wife, Sara. She enjoys cooking: the family and her husband are her priorities. Janene's lovely, just the kind of sunny personality I like around. But I wonder what other women would say about her cheeky present to A.: a sepia photograph of herself topless on stage in his play. She had to be nude but she stopped short of giving him that photograph. 'I turned chicken and nearly didn't bring this one,' she revealed, 'but Brian urged me.' Neville's wife, Emma, was wearing a beautiful blue chiffon two-piece. Had to ask about it. Jean Muir's. Another of Neville's clients!

Carol turned up in time for dessert, then spent rest of the evening raiding my fridge. A real character. Eats no breakfast, gets hungrier as the day wears on, appetite builds up till at midnight she's ravenous and turns into a fridge-raider. Was still picking the duck at one o'clock. Funny lady.

A. left today for Cambridge. Tomorrow, at unearthly hour of 9.15 a.m., he reads *Annie Wobbler* to seminar of lecturers, writers and publishers gathered from all over world by the British Council. Also wants to catch some of the other participants in action – the young playwright, Louise Page; the Jewish novelist, Howard Jacobson. So he opted to stay overnight.

These events revive his spirits; he gets enthusiastic feedback.

Another dinner party Wednesday night. Toshi Marks coming with boyfriend, Donald Pike RN. They've just come back from Japan with news of theatre director Koichi. Friends Lisa and John said they might come. Frank Ward, the food and wine writer, is here from Stockholm. And we're expecting the Japanese professor Fumika Miya. She wrote an essay on A. for a Japanese theatre magazine which devoted one of its issues to his work.

Duck with Blackcurrant Sauce

8 portions duck
2 oz / 50 g butter
1 large onion, chopped

1 pint / 600 ml chicken stock
Salt and pepper to taste
½ lb / 225 g blackcurrants

Melt butter in heavy pot. Fry onion for 5 minutes. Add duck portions and brown on both sides. Pour in stock, seasoned to taste. Cover. Simmer for 1 hour. Remove portions with slotted spoon. Keep hot. Skim as much fat from liquid as possible. Add blackcurrants. Warm through for about 10 minutes. Liquidise stock and blackcurrants. Pour over duck portions.

Pommes Lyonnaises

2 lb / 900 g potatoes, finely
   sliced
2 large onions, finely sliced
2 eggs, beaten

1 pint / 600 ml milk
2 oz / 50 g butter
Salt and pepper to taste

Butter deep ovenproof dish. Spread alternate layers of potatoes and onions, seasoning to taste between layers. Beat eggs together with milk. Pour over potatoes. Dot with butter. Cover and bake for 1 hour at 200°C / 400°F / gas mark 6. Remove cover. Bake for further 30 minutes until potatoes become crisp and brown.

If you're feeling indulgent you can use single cream instead of milk. You can grate Cheddar cheese between the layers. You can flavour with nutmeg.

Banana Flambé

4 large bananas, peeled and
   sliced lengthwise
2 oz / 50 g brown sugar
1 tablespoon lemon juice
1 teaspoon mixed spice

4 tablespoons dark rum
2 oz / 50 g butter
½ pint / 300 ml double cream,
   whipped

Lay slices of banana in shallow ovenproof dish. Sprinkle with sugar, lemon juice, mixed spice and half the rum. Dot with butter. Cover and bake at 200°C / 400°F / gas mark 6 for 20 minutes. Before serving, heat other half of rum in small frying pan and ignite. Pour flaming rum over bananas. Serve with whipped cream.

Thursday 18 July Decided to do something special with avocados - guacamole, a Mexican dish. And my old favourite – chopped liver, which turned out extra special for no reason I can offer except I used duck instead of chicken fat. That's the kind of spontaneous, unexpected ingredient which can make all the difference to a dish. Invented new chicken concoction with cheese topping. Made two desserts: dried apricots, which Yildiz brought from Turkey, soaked in brandy and served with whipped cream; and bread and butter pudding. But what a bread and butter pudding! Very moist and full of different tastes and textures. And Donald turned it down! Why? Did it remind him of unpleasant public school meals? Or 40 years of Royal Navy stodge? Not *my* bread and butter pudding! Lots of food left over. Japanese ladies have such small appetites.

Fumika, like all our Japanese friends, came laden with gifts. But she unnerved me. She arrived late, at 8.30, announced she had to catch train from Waterloo at 10.30 and I felt driven to get through a three-course meal and serve her coffee in an hour and a quarter. Then, when we lost track of time, she revealed there was a *later* train she could catch!

Into this meal-under-pressure came my darling daughter, high and fraught from an interview she'd just had for a job with literary agent Curtis Brown. Desperately wanted it but feared that, by acting too cool to counteract her natural exuberance, she might have communicated indifference. Contemplated writing letter. I strongly advised her against it. Everyone agreed with me. Frank Ward had brought his daughter. She was going to live and work in London. Tanya at once took her under her wing.

Carol, her friend Margaret and A. finished chicken dish at lunchtime today, and dug deep into the bread and butter pudding which tasted even better one day old and cold. Served the rest to Della and Ralph who came for a bite and to say goodbye to the old man. He's disappearing into his Welsh mountains to write a play, or the lyrics for his musical of *The Kitchen* – something to earn money and whittle down bank overdraft and pay for all this feeding. Lisa, John and Josh who hadn't turned up for last night's dinner also came to say goodbye. Chopped liver went, and huge dish of egg salad.

Guacamole (Avocado Salad)

2 ripe avocados
1 clove garlic, crushed
1 medium onion, finely
   chopped
1 tablespoon lemon juice
4 tomatoes, skinned, seeds
   removed, chopped

2 tablespoons parsley, chopped
Chilli pepper to taste
Freshly ground black pepper
   and salt to taste

Halve avocados. Remove stones and scoop out flesh. Put into blender with other ingredients. Serve immediately with hot toast.

Chicken with Cheese Topping

1½ lb / 675 g cooked chicken
   meat
½ lb / 225 g carrots, diced
½ lb / 225 g frozen peas
1 large onion, chopped
1 oz / 25 g butter
1 tablespoon flour

1 tablespoon tarragon
¼ pint / 150 ml milk
¼ pint / 150 ml white wine
Salt and pepper to taste
½ lb / 225 g Cheddar cheese,
   grated

Put chicken meat in ovenproof dish. Boil carrots in salted water for 10 minutes. Cook peas and add with carrots to chicken meat. Fry onions in butter. Remove with slotted spoon and lay on top of chicken. Add flour and tarragon to butter and make a roux. Let out with milk and wine to make a creamy sauce. Season to taste. Pour over chicken meat. Sprinkle grated cheese on top. Bake for 20 minutes at 190°C / 375°F / gas mark 5.

Bread and Butter Pudding

12 slices of buttered bread,
   crusts removed
Grated rind of 1 lemon
Grated rind of 1 orange
½ pint / 300 ml single cream

2 eggs, separated
6 oz / 175 g sugar
½ teaspoon vanilla
2 oz / 50 g flaked almonds,
   toasted

Butter baking tin, about 12 × 8 in / 30 × 20 cm. Layer slices of bread and butter, scattering lemon and orange rind between each layer. Mix cream, egg yolks, sugar and vanilla. Whip egg whites till stiff.

Fold into egg mix. Pour over bread. Sprinkle flaked almonds on top. Bake at 180°C / 350°F / gas mark 4 for about 30 minutes.

Do not allow to overcook. Best eaten moist. Also delicious cold.

Saturday 27 July

Back to the flat lands where I spent my first twenty years. The draw of city life is strong but this countryside will always have a hold on me. Left behind many early loves. Thirty years ago!

My plan is to spend today taking Mum out on trips. Tomorrow we'll pick raspberries so I can drive straight back to London and get them into the freezer. Mum and I always pick fruit at a farm near where she lives by the river. She says: 'When we're fed up with picking fruit, we can fish for trout!' Us! Raspberry canes very high. Picking is like a game of hide and seek. We call to each other every so often to check how full our containers are and then I make a journey back to have them weighed and put in the shade. Normally pick about 40 lb but 1985 has been a disaster for the crop. Lack of sunshine. Didn't ripen until very late.

Sunday 28 July

Mum was so anxious about weather she was up at 5 a.m., holding her hand out of the window to see if it was raining. Did, of course, as so many days this year. Picking between showers not the best way to pick soft fruit! Collected about 24 lb, still enough to make raspberry Pavlovas and hosts of other delicious dishes. Mum said she would pick more the following days and make jam for me. She's marvellous at it and, like me, a compulsive picker when she gets the opportunity. Some years we've been known to stay picking for many hours with the sun beating down on us until we were so weak from hunger we'd rush home and fall on thick chunks of bread with cheese. Had good times and laughed a lot, she and me.

Saturday night, took her out for dinner to a pub which had recently been taken over by one of her neighbours – an ex-Squadron Leader. Amazed to discover his daughter, who was in her early twenties, had undertaken to run a kitchen which served 100 lunches on a Sunday. Her mother, a teacher, was her only help. She cooked the joints on a Saturday night in such a way that she could re-heat the meat on the Sunday. Can't understand how they could do that satisfactorily.

Ben Shaktman arrives from Dallas tomorrow. Rang from there this afternoon. Said:

'An idea crossed my mind. Wouldn't it make more sense if you came to the airport to pick me up and we went straight on to Wales?'

'Yes,' I replied. 'What time does your plane arrive?'

'6 a.m.,' he informed me.

'Forget it,' I said. Wonder how he takes jet lag. My plan is to let him grab a few hours sleep and then be on the road in time to reach A. and the Black Mountains for dinner.

Known Ben for years. In 1973 Joe Papp asked him to direct *The Old Ones* in his New York Public Theatre. Joe and Ben had disagreed over Ben's ideas. Joe turned up on the first day of rehearsal and announced the production was cancelled. Just like that. Ben went on to do a workshop production. Well received, but died. He ran the Pittsburg Public Theatre for ten years, worked in other fields, now was restless. Plans to start work on a new play. Hopes Wales will inspire him. Writing was his first love. He'd obtained a Fulbright scholarship to study theatre in Bristol in the 60s.

Whenever I go to Wales, take as much food as possible from London because resent paying inflated prices of our nearest town, Hay-on-Wye. Decided I'd half-cook some chicken pieces and bake a couple of cakes for midnight raiding. Had a second go at pecan and prune to make sure I'd got it right, then baked an old favourite, marmalade cake, adding egg white this time, as an experiment. Made it lighter.

Marmalade Cake

6 oz / 175 g butter
6 oz / 175 g sugar
3 eggs, separated
2 oz / 50 g chopped mixed peel
Grated rind of 1 orange

3 tablespoons chunky
  marmalade
10 oz / 275 g self-raising flour
5 tablespoons water

Butter 8 in / 20 cm tin. Cream butter and sugar. Add egg yolks, mixed peel, orange rind and marmalade. Fold in flour. Gradually work in water. Beat egg whites till stiff. Fold in. Bake at 190°c / 375°f / gas mark 5 for about 45 minutes or until knife comes out clean.

Monday
5 August

Ben arrived on time. Came through door, hugged life out of me, went straight to kitchen, sat at the table like a child waiting to be fed and said: 'Hello! I'm here again!'

He showered and I put him to bed in my bed. Didn't want to disturb clean sheets of other beds I'd prepared for further guests due to arrive the following weekend. Half-cooked chickens, baked apricot upside-down cake, went out shopping. Four hours later woke him up and offered him a selection of things for a light lunch. Reminded me he was a vegetarian! Christ! all that chicken. A. and I will have to eat it for days! Made him scrambled eggs.

On the way down showed him our special Cotswold village of Burford where he insisted on sampling a scone and cream tea and on being photographed up and down the High Street. He bubbled with questions and enthusiasm. 'What I love about Bishops Road is sitting in the kitchen and watching an endless stream of people in different states of dress come in and out.' I enjoy people like Ben. They're rewarding in their appreciation of every tiny incident. Thought jet lag might send him to sleep on journey. Not Ben. We gossiped a lot and his eyes were all over the landscape.

He had great difficulty in comprehending our postal system. If Herefordshire was in England and Breconshire was in Wales and Hay was in Breconshire then why was our postal address 'Hay-on-Wye, Hereford?' Only the flies bothered him. He had a thing about flies. Nothing, though, seemed to diminish his pleasure in what he saw – the hills, the patchwork fields, 'all those hedges', the vistas, the cottage of which I was reasonably proud though I wish we had money to do more work on it. His pleasure pleased me. But I confessed to him: my heart is really with the sea. I grew up with fields. I want the wide ocean.

Arrived around six in time for 'happy hour'. In this most dreadful of all summers (God! how I yearn for some sun) we arrived on an unusually bright day. Armed with vodka and tonic at once set about preparing dinner. A. was starving. He's on strict diet when alone and working. As soon as I arrive, he falls on everything. Was glad I'd brought lots of fresh vegetables and cheese, but once I'd laid the chicken on the table Ben said:

'I do allow myself a little bit of chicken sometimes, and as this looks and smells so good I'm going to indulge myself.' Just as well because he was horrified to hear that he could eat fish only on Thursday, market day in Hay. Can see I'm going to have to rack my brains concocting vegetarian dishes for him.

Chicken with Peanut Sauce

6 joints of chicken

Salt and pepper to taste

Season chicken joints. Grill for 20 minutes on each side under medium heat. Transfer to serving dish. Keep warm.

Peanut sauce

2 tablespoons crunchy peanut butter
1 small onion, grated
1 clove garlic, crushed
1 teaspoon honey, clear

1 dessertspoon lemon juice
1 dessertspoon soya sauce
1 tablespoon single cream
1 tablespoon water
Watercress to garnish

While chickens grill, put all sauce ingredients in saucepan and stir over low heat until creamy in consistency. Pour over grilled chicken pieces. Garnish with watercress, for colour.

Apricot Upside-Down Cake

4 oz / 100 g butter
4 oz / 100 g castor sugar
2 large eggs, beaten

Grated rind 1 lemon
4 oz / 100 g self-raising flour
½ teaspoon baking powder

Topping

1 oz / 25 g butter
3 oz / 75 g soft brown sugar

15 oz / 425 g fresh apricots, halved and pipped

Grease 8 in / 20 cm loose-bottomed tin.

Make topping first. Melt butter, add sugar and stir over gentle heat. Spread over base of tin. Lay apricots on top, cut side up.

The cake next: cream butter and sugar. Add eggs and lemon rind. Fold in flour and baking powder. Spoon mixture over apricots. Make sure it's level. Bake at 170°C / 325°F / gas mark 3 for 50 minutes.

Friday
9 August

Great surprise! Hadn't been in the door five minutes, having returned from shopping spree in Hay, when another car hooted its way up to the gate. Lindsay Joe with two musicians. He had to be in Cardiff to hear a group playing, and to sign up this couple – a black female singer and her white composer/accompanist – from Bristol. 'I was so near I thought we'd come to lunch.' Had a big fry-up ready for them within the half-hour – eggs, rashers, tinned baked beans, the day's fresh bread, home-made jam, marmalade cake, and a bowl of fresh raspberries which we'd picked the day before, covered with lashings of cream. Two hours later they were gone, clutching a bottle each of my jams over which they'd done so much oohing and aahing that I couldn't resist giving them as presents.

Have spent the last few days trying but failing to feed an amusing but sick man. Well, not really sick, but Ben had eaten a tuna-fish sandwich in Dallas and come away with an upset stomach. Complicated my plans for his special vegetarian dishes. Thank God it's summer (at least in name), so could present him with fresh salads on Tuesday. For Wednesday offered him sesame rice fritters and stuffed aubergines but even this was worrying to him. He ate only half of one. We had not simply a vegetarian on our hands but a finicky one! Was rather pleased with my aubergines, though.

Last night invited across the fields to the Browne-Wilkinsons, Percy and Nicho. Their house-guests were Percy's niece, an actress, and her husband who runs the Contact Theatre in Manchester. They

so frequently ask A. over for dinner when he's here on his own that we feel a little guilty. Rang Percy to ask could I make the dessert.

'Do you desperately want to cook?' she asked me.

'Yes,' I replied. 'I feel in the mood.' Made raspberry Pavlova, adding wild strawberries from the garden as an extra decoration.

A.'s very proud of his exotic little fruit. Found a small cluster outside back door when we first moved in 15 years ago. Since then he's tended them and put cuttings all over the place. How they spread! Was very insistent I used them somehow, but he'd soaked them in gin! Didn't help! Also took them my blackcurrant and raspberry jam. Percy joined in spoiling Ben by concocting a vegetarian meal in his honour – sorrel and spinach soup, quiche Lorraine, mangetouts and new potatoes.

I admire Percy's energy. She had five children, packed them off on their own when they were of age, sold up her London house, bought the tumble-down cottage off old man Prosser three fields from us, plus 60 acres, and set up a sheep farm. Every summer she writes to her friends inviting them to book up their weekends. Don't wonder A. enjoys his evenings with them, all sorts of interesting people move through from MPs and judges to bankers and actresses. Now they were both down, Nicho for a long spell, tending his vegetable garden. Very flourishing it is too!

Today two more of our guests arrived – Lisa and Bernie. Lisa's the daughter of A.'s ex-agent. Known her since childhood. She paints. Three years ago we took down the paintings in Bishops Road, hung her work for a week, kept open house and sold seven pictures for her. Bernie is also a fine artist. Earns his bread and butter sculpting figures for Henson of Muppets fame. They arrived laden with two bottles of champagne, two bottles each of red and white wine, and a packet of sliced smoked salmon. Deep-fried some hake and plaice and, at Ben's request, some potato latkas, one of the Jewish dishes I inherited on entry to the tribe! I also inherited a taste for my fish done in light coating. Moist, not over-cooked. Can't bear that fish and chip shop batter.

Vegetarian Stuffed Aubergines

2 large aubergines
1 onion, finely chopped
1 tablespoon vegetable oil
1 clove garlic, crushed
6 oz / 175 g mushrooms, finely
  chopped

½ green pepper, diced
2 tomatoes, skinned and
  chopped
Salt and pepper to taste
6 oz / 175 g Cheddar cheese,
  grated for topping

Bake aubergines in oven until soft. Fry onion in oil. Add all other ingredients except cheese. Simmer for 20 minutes. Halve aubergines lengthwise. Carefully remove flesh from skins. Mix with cooked vegetables. Return mixture to aubergine skins. Sprinkle grated cheese on top. Bake in oven at 180°C / 350°F / gas mark 4 for 10 minutes.

Potato Latkas

4 large potatoes, grated and very
  well drained
1 large onion, grated
2 large eggs, beaten

4 oz / 100 g fine matzo meal
1 teaspoon salt
½ teaspoon white pepper
Oil for frying

Mix all ingredients. Form into little cakes. Fry for 10 minutes on each side in hot oil. Drain on kitchen paper.

Sesame Rice Fritters

6 oz / 175 g cooked brown rice
1 egg, separated, plus 1 egg yolk
2 tablespoons whole wheat flour
1 teaspoon salt
Pinch of pepper

2 oz / 50 g toasted, ground
  sesame seeds
2 tablespoons milk
Oil for frying

Mix together rice, 2 egg yolks, flour, salt and pepper, ground sesame seeds and milk. Beat egg white till stiff. Fold in. Heat oil. Drop tablespoons of mixture into hot oil, a few at a time, fry until brown. Drain on kitchen paper.

Fried Hake

12 hake cutlets
8 oz / 225 g medium
  matzo meal

6 eggs, beaten
Vegetable oil for frying
Salt and pepper to taste

Coat hake cutlets in matzo meal. Dip into seasoned beaten egg. Just
before frying, roll in matzo meal once more. Fry in deep hot oil, 10
minutes each side. Drain on kitchen paper.

This coating can be used on all fried fish.

Lisa and Bernie left before lunch. A good weekend. Discovered Ben *Monday*
was not only a finicky vegetarian fearful for his stomach, he was *12 August*
anxious about his body in general. Spent Saturday afternoon at
Llanigon agricultural show organised by the Young Farmers'
Association. Love such events, full of prize-winning sheep, cattle and
horses which people spend days cleaning and grooming.

Drove on to show our guests surrounding countryside. Up to
Abergavenny and back through mountain roads to stunning Llan-
tony Abbey. Stopped for drinks and more photographs of Ben among
the ruins. At the Gospel Pass Bernie and A. got out to walk the last
lap. Ben declined. On arrival at the house realised that A. had the
front door key. Only way into house was up a ladder and through a
small bedroom window some ten feet off the ground which I'd
thankfully left open. Ben said:

'Well, we'll just have to wait won't we?'

'No,' I replied. 'We'll get the ladder and you'll have to climb
through.'

'I can't climb up ladders,' he protested.

'I've never known anyone as wet as you,' Lisa told him. She
shamed him into making the dangerous ascent. But he had to be
photographed.

'So's my friends will believe I did it!'

That night we got our dinner off the smoked salmon, scrambled
eggs, a huge salad which Lisa put together, and the champagne.

Made an old-fashioned Sunday lunch for Sunday dinner to which
we returned from another day's outing. This time in the Brecon
Beacons. Visited a hidden waterfall into which Ben refused to
descend. 'Not me, baby!' Warned everyone it would be a late dinner
but worth waiting for. Cheese soufflé, roast beef – topside, roast
potatoes, french beans, carrots and Yorkshire puddings which for
Ben's sake I made with batter in a buttered dish. He got his dinner off
those, the vegetables, cheese and a dessert of blackcurrant sorbet.

Hope Ben's not coming through as a drag. Far from it. I love him.
He's not only great fun, he's an enthusiast. Everything pleased him

and all his complaining was shaped as much to amuse us as anything else. Tonight will offer him a herb-stuffed marrow. They're in season and seeing them at the Llanigon show gave me an appetite for them. Feel marrow is a very neglected vegetable. I love it. Sometimes just dice it, steam it, and serve with simple onion sauce. Used to make it with mince for A. Haven't done so for years. Treat for them both.

Marrow Stuffed with Herbs

1 small marrow
1 small onion, chopped
2 oz / 50 g butter
4 oz / 100 g fresh white
  breadcrumbs
4 oz / 100 g unsalted peanuts,
  crushed

1 teaspoon parsley
2 teaspoons tarragon
1 egg, beaten
Salt and pepper to taste

Fry onion in butter. Mix in other ingredients. Cut end off marrow and carefully remove seeds. Fill cavity with mixture. Wrap in buttered foil. Bake at 180°C / 350°F / gas mark 4 for 45 minutes. Serve sliced.

Cheese Soufflé

4 oz / 100 g butter
4 oz / 100 g plain flour
½ pint / 300 ml milk
6 eggs, separated

6 oz / 175 g Cheddar cheese
Salt and pepper to taste
1 teaspoon cayenne pepper

Grease 8 in / 20 cm soufflé dish.

Melt butter. Stir in flour to make roux. Let out with milk until a thick sauce. Remove from heat. Beat in egg yolks. Stir in cheese. Season to taste. Whip egg whites till stiff. Fold in to mixture and pour into dish. Sprinkle cayenne pepper on top. Bake at 200°C / 400°F / gas mark 6 for about 30 minutes.

Blackcurrant Sorbet

8 oz / 225 g blackcurrants	½ pint / 300 ml water
½ teaspoon gelatine	4 oz / 100 g castor sugar
2 teaspoons lemon juice	1 egg white, stiffly beaten

Dissolve gelatine in lemon juice. Heat water and gently dissolve sugar. Then boil for 10 minutes until syrupy. Add blackcurrants and simmer for 10 minutes. Cool slightly. Purée blackcurrants and stir in gelatine. Put into blender for 3 minutes. Pour into bowl. Fold in egg white. Pour into ramekins. Chill before serving.

This is going to be a packed, long weekend. I feel it. Started already. *Thursday* Last night. Monday was the last of my Welsh meals because on *15 August* Tuesday Percy again invited us over for dinner, with her guests – two of our oldest friends, Jim and Pam Rose. We used to take the children for the day to their cottage in East Grinstead. They still have marks on their door measuring the children's growth. Strange, or perhaps not so strange, that they and the Browne-Wilkinsons should be mutual friends. Thought I'd take one of my walnut cakes.

Come back to London yesterday. Left Ben to get on with his play. He made endless jokes about being abandoned and how would he manage. Filled fridge with salad, cheese, a pot of vegetable soup, yoghurts, eggs, bread. Demanded I leave the rest of the marmalade and pecan cakes. A. showed him how to operate heating system. Warned him the first hours after we'd gone he'd feel very sad.

Arrived in London around 2.30. A painful journey. A. lost his temper over a triviality. Often happens when we leave the Welsh hills for London. I'm happy to be returning, he hates it. I'd invited the children to have dinner with us. Turned out to be a full house with two French friends, a Turkish one, and an unexpected guest – A.'s

60-year-old eccentric cousin who'd not been to see us in years. On my first evening home! One I'd set aside for my children and sorely missed grand-daughter. Packed him off upstairs to A. in the study. He was only answering his mail. Let *him* cope!

Didn't make anything special, just chicken and mushroom crêpes (see page 57), lots of it. And baked fresh fruit as a *brûlé*. This time of year is lovely for fresh fruits. Peaches and apricots, covered with rum and brown sugar, served with whipped cream and cookies. Simple. Can't think why but A. remarked how tasty they were. Meal overwhelmed by cousin Ralph who loudly smacked his lips, sucked his teeth and disjointedly talked in between his strange laughter. He thrust at A. a book of Hackney poets containing three of his poems and insisted he listen to a tape of piano music he'd composed. Our guests were mesmerised. I was paralysed. When the tape went on, left A. and French friend to listen. The rest of us fled to the kitchen.

A story about how one of my dinner parties came about. A. wrote *Annie Wobbler* for Nichola McAuliffe. Nichola is now in a play called *State Of Affairs* directed by Peter James who runs the Lyric Theatre, Hammersmith. Peter is trying to turn the Lyric into a theatre with a reputation for presenting work of foreign directors and actors. He invited Nuria Espert, the great Spanish actress, to direct Glenda Jackson in a Lorca play. Nuria declined, mainly out of terror, it transpired. She'd only ever co-directed. Nichola told Peter that we knew Nuria, adding she was sure A. could persuade Nuria to come to London at least to meet and have exploratory talks with Glenda and Peter and to view the theatre. Nichola rang A. in Wales. A. wrote to Nuria in Madrid. Nuria rang from Barcelona a couple of hours ago. She'll come. 'I will hold you responsible for the catastrophe,' she told him. Glenda, Nuria and Peter will all meet for the first time round my table at dinner. I've already decided what to cook – pheasant in sherry sauce.

2 oz / 50 g butter
1 onion, chopped
2 leeks, sliced
1 pint / 600 ml water
½ lb / 225 g carrots

2 sticks celery, chopped
1 tablespoon parsley, chopped
½ lb / 225 g pearl barley
Salt and pepper to taste
¼ pint / 150 ml single cream

In a large saucepan melt butter and fry onions and leeks for 10 minutes. Add water, remaining vegetables and parsley and barley. Simmer gently until barley is cooked, about 30 minutes. Season. Add cream just before serving.

Walnut Cake

4 oz / 100 g butter
2 tablespoons golden syrup
2 oz / 50 g brown sugar
3 eggs, separated

4 oz / 100 g self-raising flour
2 oz / 50 g chopped walnuts
¼ pint / 150 ml milk

Cream butter, golden syrup and brown sugar. Beat in egg yolks, one at a time. Fold in flour and chopped walnuts. Add milk to make mixture of an even consistency. Fold in beaten egg whites. Bake at 190°C / 375°F / gas mark 5 for 40 minutes.

Fruit Brûlé

3 lb / 1.3 kg mixed fruit, such as
    peaches, apricots,
    strawberries and cherries,
    halved and pipped
4 oz / 100 g castor sugar
½ pint / 300 ml water

3 tablespoons kirsch
¾ pint / 400 ml double cream,
    whipped
6 oz / 175 g brown sugar for
    topping

Place fruit, castor sugar and water in saucepan. Poach for 10 minutes. Drain and pour into shallow ovenproof dish. Add kirsch. Spread whipped cream on top. Sprinkle brown sugar over cream. Grill until sugar melts and cream begins to bubble. Best served hot.

Friday **My American house-guests have taken A. to see a lovely film called**
16 August *Witness.* I'd seen it on my own one evening when he was in Wales.
Just my kind of film. I'm fascinated by the preservation of times past
– whether it's a TV documentary about an Indian tribe in the
Amazon struggling to survive in the twentieth century, or a religious
sect like the Amish of Pennsylvania in the film, persisting with their
simple beliefs and habits surrounded by so much commercialism,
living without radios or telephones in a technological age. Not sure I
could do that, though.

Our guests, Gerry Crogan, a therapist, and his boyfriend Lewis, an
architect, were the main reason for our returning from Wales.
They're here for three days before going on to Sicily. Gerry had
entertained me very well in New York. Asked me to make a dinner
party for him. 'Invite somebody interesting.' God knows how you
can judge who'll be interesting to whom. I certainly never can. Just
invited people I like or hadn't seen for some time, such as Gary Bond
who created the role of Pip in *Chips With Everything*, and was now
starring with Nichola in *State Of Affairs*. Nichola, as well, of course.
And Pamela Howard, who might turn up late because she's designed
Taming Of The Shrew for an RSC tour and they're lighting. And Lisa
and John – at least John, an academic psychologist, might have
something in common with Gerry. And Shusha whom we'd introduced to Gerry. They were now great buddies. And my children. For
next Sunday.

Gerry had said he liked pork. Decided to roast a hand of pork in
honey. Lewis had said he liked fish. Thought I'd try monkfish in
white wine sauce. But for this evening roasted them a leg of lamb.
Had it wrapped in tin foil in the fridge for 24 hours marinating with
garlic, lots of mint, salt and pepper. For dessert a closed peach and
blueberry pie in almond pastry. Gerry had two portions. L.J. came to
do his washing. Demolished the rest. If the boys are looking forward
to more when they return from the cinema they'll be disappointed. It
was good, even if I say so myself.

4 lb / 1.8 kg leg of lamb	1 tablespoon soya sauce
2 tablespoons mint, chopped	1 tablespoon clear honey
1 tablespoon chopped onion	1 tablespoon tomato purée
2 cloves garlic, crushed	1 pint / 600 ml red wine
1 teaspoon olive oil	1 tablespoon arrowroot
Salt and black pepper to taste	

Trim excess fat from lamb. Make deep incisions under skin. Push in chopped mint, onions and garlic wherever possible. Rub all over with olive oil and season with salt and pepper. Place in baking tin. Stir soya sauce, honey and tomato purée into red wine. Pour over lamb. Wrap in tin foil and leave for 24 hours before cooking. Turn occasionally.

To cook: drain off red wine and retain. Roast meat at 200°C /400°F / gas mark 6 for 1½ hours. Mix meat juices with red wine, thickening with arrowroot, to make gravy.

Peach and Blueberry Pie in Almond Pastry

Almond pastry

4 oz / 100 g butter	3 oz / 75 g castor sugar
6 oz / 175 g plain flour	Grated rind of lemon
2½ oz / 70 g ground almonds	2 egg yolks

Rub butter into flour and ground almonds. Add sugar and grated lemon rind. Bind with egg yolk and roll into a ball. Keep in cool place for half an hour.

Grease 10 in / 25 cm flan tin. Line with pastry. Bake blind at 190°C / 375°F / gas mark 5 for 15 minutes.

Filling

15 oz / 425 g tin peach halves in fruit juice, not syrup	1 tablespoon castor sugar
	2 tablespoons ground almonds
15 oz / 425 g tin blueberries	2 eggs
1 pint / 600 ml sour cream	1 teaspoon vanilla

Drain peaches and blueberries and lay on pastry. Blend sour cream, sugar, ground almonds, eggs and vanilla. Spoon over the fruit. Bake at 180°C / 350°F / gas mark 4 for 30 minutes.

Monday
19 August

Was grateful to be heading for Wales again after hectic weekend in Bishops Road. Every bed – including divan in TV room – was occupied. Both bathrooms constantly busy. Eight is my favourite number round a table, but it's often not possible. People are always dropping in. Fifteen for Gerry's dinner. An interesting mix. Which is not to say everyone absolutely adored everyone else. There were some amusing tensions in the most unexpected quarters. But chatter was unceasing, lots of loud laughter and – most important for me – gusts of approval each time I announced a dish. As usual gave them choices and as usual most shouted out they wanted to sample everything. Had to call for order with each new course. An unruly lot but rewarding.

The starters grew out of my Saturday morning shop. Had no ideas until I saw a display of button mushrooms in Waitrose. Can't resist the tiny things. Marinated they make an excellent starter. Also in Waitrose, my beady eyes found large fresh prawns and ripe honeydew melons. When you see these things you have to buy them because there they are, ready to eat! Unlike avocados, which I used with the prawns and melon (served in vinaigrette), but which I'd had for the past four days waiting around to ripen.

For dessert a cheesecake, but with a difference. Instead of decorating the top with mandarins took a risk and folded them into the cheese mixture. Prayed it wouldn't curdle. Didn't! Always cook with my fingers crossed! And into the graham cracker base added crushed pecans. Why not! Second dessert was an open peaches and nectarine pie with a base of graham crackers which, this time, I put on the top. Why not! Gerry, who'd been out for coffee, lunch *and* tea, ate his way through everything.

At about 11.45 there was a knock at the front door. Carol! (She'd threatened she'd gatecrash in time for dessert.) Surrounded by five cases, irritatingly suntanned, and bedecked with a new hair style of corn strands, our own Jewish Bo Derek! 'I've been arrested,' she announced without moving from the doorstep. She'd been stopped at Heathrow. Every case had been thoroughly searched. She'd had a body check. Carol is not a smoker, but they found an old pipe she'd bought in Paris as a souvenir which still had traces of someone else's pot! It was a technical arrest. She was trying to make the event dramatic, but I suspect they let her go because she talked them into fatigue. The search should only have taken an hour. It took five.

Now she waded into the left-overs and, feeling rather high on her experience, stayed up till the early hours in the TV room where she watched and wept over A.'s play on video, *Love Letters On Blue Paper*. My favourite too. Managed to rescue some cheesecake to bring back to Wales for Ben. He was very grateful. Leapt into my arms on arrival. Mother had returned! Took him out for dinner together with A.'s godson, Jonathan, whom we'd brought back with us. 'Mother' couldn't face any more cooking. This morning A. got up at 6.15 in order to drive Ben to Hay to catch the bus for Hereford. He's off to the South of France and sun. Not fair!

One of the messages on our answering machine was from a dramaturge of the Thalia theatre in Hamburg. A. asked me if he could invite him for Sunday lunch when we return. That's how gatherings grow.

Now I have the children to look forward to. Not Daniel, who's working, but Lindsay and Magda who've promised to come with Natasha and Tanya for August bank holiday weekend. If they change their minds I shall be so disappointed. Can't help it, they're really all I care about in the end.

Marinated Mushrooms

1½ lb / 675 g baby mushrooms
2 tablespoons vegetable oil
2 cloves garlic, crushed
1 large onion, finely chopped
½ pint / 300 ml dry white wine
2 bay leaves

2 tablespoons chopped parsley
1 dessertspoon coriander seeds, crushed
1 teaspoon ground black pepper
Salt to taste

Using deep pan, cook garlic and onion in oil for 5 minutes on medium heat. Stir in wine, herbs, pepper and salt. Add mushrooms. Cook for 5 minutes. Turn into bowl. Chill before serving.

Mandarin Cheesecake

3 oz / 75 g butter, melted
4 oz / 100 g graham crackers, crushed
8 oz / 225 g pecan nuts, crushed
2 × 10½ oz / 298 g tins mandarin oranges, drained

¼ pint / 150 ml sour cream
1 lb / 450 g curd cheese
6 oz / 175 g castor sugar
3 eggs
½ teaspoon vanilla

Grease 9 in / 22 cm loose-bottomed cake tin.

Mix melted butter with crushed Graham Crackers. Add crushed pecans. Press half into loose-bottomed tin. Lay oranges on top. Blend cream, cheese, sugar, eggs and vanilla. Pour over oranges. Sprinkle remainder of crackers and pecans on top. Bake at 180°C / 350°F / gas mark 4 for 35 minutes or until set.

Peach and Nectarine Pie

1 lb / 450 g shortcrust pastry	1 tablespoon Grand Marnier
6 large peaches, peeled and sliced	3 tablespoons flour
	6 oz / 175 g sugar
6 large nectarines, peeled and sliced	1 teaspoon cinnamon
	1 teaspoon arrowroot
1 tablespoon lemon juice	

Soak fruit in Grand Marnier and lemon juice for half an hour.

Grease deep 10 in / 25 cm pie dish. Line with half the pastry.

Mix flour, sugar and cinnamon. Remove half the fruit with slotted spoon and place in pie base. Sprinkle on half the sugar and flour mix. Add another layer of fruit. Sprinkle with remaining sugar and flour mix. Thicken juice with arrowroot. Pour over fruit. Cover with remaining pastry. Prick top and bake at 200°C / 400°F / gas mark 6 for 10 minutes, then at 180°C / 350°F / gas mark 4 for further 40 minutes.

Monkfish in White Wine

2 large monkfish tails, skinned	1/2 pint / 300 ml fish stock
4 oz / 100 g butter	1/2 pint / 300 ml white wine
2 large leeks, sliced	2 tablespoons flour
4 oz / 100 g mushrooms, chopped	2 egg yolks, beaten
	1/4 pint / 150 ml cream
2 large carrots, sliced	Salt and pepper to taste

Using large heavy-bottomed pot, melt 3 oz / 75 g butter. Fry leeks, mushrooms and carrots for 10 minutes. Lay fish tails in pot (either whole or cut into portions). Pour in wine and fish stock. Cover and cook for 30 minutes. Remove fish with slotted spoon. Keep warm. Similarly remove vegetables. Keep apart and warm.

Using medium-sized saucepan, melt remaining butter. Add flour to make roux. Let out gradually with liquid from fish until a creamy

sauce. Add beaten yolks, cream, salt and pepper. Pour sauce over
fish. Use vegetables to garnish.

Roast Pork in Honey

Large hand of pork	4 oz / 100 g sultanas
Seasoning to taste	2 tablespoons clear honey
¼ pint / 150 ml water	
6 medium eating apples, peeled and sliced	

Season pork. Place in baking tin with water. Arrange apples and
sultanas around meat. Spoon honey over the pork. Cook for 1½ hours
at 180°C / 350°F / gas mark 4, basting with juices from meat while it
cooks. When cooked, slice meat and garnish with sultanas and apples.
Skim excess fat off juices and spoon over meat before serving.

Wales is where we wind down and play games. Or rather *they* wind *Friday*
down. I get restless. Can't help it. Had to drive out with Jonathan. *23 August*
Visited the seaport towns of Swansea and Port Talbot. My God,
they're so depressing. Barren and grey. Lunched off scampi and
chips. Visited a Victorian folly called Coch Castle. Made the day
worthwhile.

Sit here waiting for the children. Plan was for L.J. to leave his
office to pick up Magda and the baby at 7 p.m., then pick up Tanya in
Bishops Road. I phoned. It seems they didn't get on the road till
about 9.15. We sit waiting and of course worrying about them.

They've come and gone and it was lovely. We're scheduled to return *Tuesday*
on Thursday. I wanted to return today. Compromised with A. We'll *27 August*
leave tomorrow.

They arrived last Friday at 1 a.m. What a joy to have that child in
my arms! She makes me forget this rainy, grey climate. Tanya and
Magda love it here. Lindsay used to, now seems restless. He and
Magda drove to Coventry on Saturday to listen to a pop group.
Returned 2 a.m. next morning. Had to sleep in their bed so's to keep
an eye on Natasha.

Made a huge chicken pilaff for Saturday night; barbecue on
Sunday. Tried out a new recipe for crêpes using egg whites.

Tanya was looking beautiful. Had to tell her. She grins coyly, says,

'Thank you.' Took herself off for a long talk with Percy whom she admires. Percy is wise. Wanted to talk about her old school-friend, M., a black boy serving three years for robbery, whom she's befriended, writes to and visits in the Isle of Wight. Generous soul. Worry and fear she'll be abused.

Lindsay passed the time typing out Magda's play. He tried to read A.'s new play. Couldn't get beyond scene thirteen. 'This isn't theatre, it's philosophy!' After which ensued a long, heated exchange. Enjoy listening to them. L.J. really scolds. A. takes it very well. From all of us actually. We're always telling him we don't like this or that, advising what won't work. Most people imagine a writer's surrounded by sycophants. Not this one!

Games of Scrabble, Foil, Moviemaker, Monopoly. One game bought over ten years ago we've never attempted – Diplomacy. Looks so complicated. Also warned it destroyed relationships.

We've rescued last of six early nineteenth-century heavy-bottomed ship's tumblers. Five were broken by guests who've never owned up. Taking the last one back to Bishops Road.

Chicken Pilaff

1 large onion, finely chopped	1 pint / 600 ml chicken stock
1 dessertspoon vegetable oil	8 oz / 225 g cooked chicken, chopped
4 oz / 100 g mushrooms, finely chopped	4 oz / 100 g flaked almonds
1 clove garlic, crushed	2 oz / 50 g butter
12 oz / 350 g brown rice	2 oz / 50 g raisins, soaked in hot water
1 teaspoon turmeric	
1 teaspoon cumin	8 oz / 225 g frozen peas
Salt and pepper to taste	8 oz / 225 g frozen beans

Using heavy-bottomed large casserole, fry onion in oil. Add mushrooms. Add garlic, rice, spices, and season to taste. Add stock. Bring to boil, cover and simmer for 40 minutes. Meanwhile lightly fry chopped chicken and almonds in butter. When the rice is cooked, mix in the chicken and almonds and add raisins. Add the cooked peas and beans.

½ pint / 300 ml milk
3 eggs, separated
1 tablespoon castor sugar
3 tablespoons rum

5 oz / 150 g flour
2 oz / 50 g melted butter
½ pint / 300 ml double cream,
  whipped

Place all ingredients in liquidiser except egg whites, 2 tablespoons
rum and the cream. Blend at top speed for 2 minutes. Pour into bowl.
Add pinch of salt to egg whites and beat until stiff. Fold into mixture.
Leave to rest for 2 hours.

When crêpes are cooked, layer them with rum
sprinkled in between. Serve with whipped cream.
Alternatively, serve with rum and whipped cream
separately.

A. left for Stockholm this afternoon. Invited to face press and
audience for Royal Dramaten's production of *Love Letters On Blue
Paper*. He'll also give a couple of readings of *Annie Wobbler*, to drum
up interest in the play. Packed his own case. Gone the days when I
folded each shirt and trouser leg between sheets of tissue paper.

*Tuesday
3 September*

Met A. at airport. Told him:
  'I've got one piece of bad news.'
  'Which production has been cancelled?' he asked, that being the
normal bad news.
  'No production's been cancelled. Margaret Windham's husband is
dead.'
  He was stunned. Her mother had phoned this morning. Margaret
and Michael returned last night from a holiday in Ireland, went for a

*Saturday
7 September*

meal in their local Chinese restaurant. Three drunks lumbered in. Irish labourers. Michael, being Irish, was particularly upset. Complained twice to the manager. One drunk stood up, punched him so hard he never regained consciousness. Margaret had wanted us to know.

Next came merely irritating news. The Lyric Theatre, Hammersmith, seems to have made a balls-up of the Espert/Jackson dinner. Nuria arrives Tuesday, imagining she's dining here with Glenda. Arranged with Peter James over four weeks ago. He seems not to have informed Glenda. She'll be invited now. At impossibly short notice. Will never understand why people don't take arrangements as seriously as we do. A. angry. He'd been responsible for persuading Nuria to come over. What trust will she place in the theatre's back-up?

He rang at once. Spoke to administrator, Robert Cogo-Fawcett. What was happening? Robert had just returned from holiday, wasn't too sure himself. He'd speak to Peter. Is my dinner party still on? I've bought the pheasants!

Sunday
8 September

Crossed river to Stockwell to visit Margaret. Passed Peter Woodthorpe, the actor, on his way out to do the shopping. Margaret lying stunned in bed. Mother, sister, friends keeping watch from downstairs. A painful encounter. What do you say? Showed her photos of Natasha; gossiped about this and that, passed away time hoping to distract her, show her she's not alone. Bought gooiest cake possible from Louis in Hampstead.

From sad bedside drove on to happy event – John Osborne's annual party in his huge house in Edenbridge. He's lost weight. Thought he was not looking too well. Saw lots of old acquaintances: Thelma and Peter Nichols; Alan Bates and his huge handsome twins; Donald Trelford on crutches from playing cricket. Collected food from marquee and sat with Donald. He introduced us to a drunk journalist who couldn't wait to tell A.: 'Oh, Wesker, you once wrote a play about the Air Force or something. I gave it a bad review in the *Radio Times*.' That's why we prefer dinner parties at home. Go out and you never know which sour, disappointed soul lurks waiting to take a swipe.

Situation worsens. Glenda Jackson's agent can't get hold of her though he's certain she'll be free, she's expressed such interest in the project. Still can't be sure whom I'm cooking for. Nor can they find a hotel for Nuria. Said we'd have her with pleasure but they must ask her first. We're old friends, but some people prefer hotels rather than private houses in which they feel obligated.

They rang back. She was delighted to stay in Bishops Road, which she remembers warmly from the time we entertained her company. Good! One problem solved.

Next problem – who would meet her? Not a problem really, A. had planned to be there. But no one seemed to have thought about it at the theatre. He told them they *had* to be there, and with flowers!

Glenda not coming to dinner. She'll meet Nuria at 11 a.m. on Thursday at the theatre. What the hell is Nuria supposed to do until then? A. is furious. Feels he's been made to seem unreliable. Rang theatre and told them they'd better have a good explanation for their visitor. He's just rushed off to airport with last of the roses from the garden.

This damn journal! Can't find time to write it. So much happening. Decided to accept an invitation to go to Germany for first night of *Their Very Own And Golden City* in Brunswick. They offered to pay A.'s flight. He's asked them to add a few pounds to cover car and ferry instead, so we can both go. A little adventure! Between cooking, I've been ringing RAC, buying maps, looking for car insurance and log-book which I'd put in a safe place and can't find!

It's taken days to recover from summer holiday in winter Wales. All that gloom! And a back-log of mail to catch up with.

Magda – stage name Jaqueline Rudet – has two plays scheduled for the Theatre Upstairs at the Royal Court, our old stomping ground. Rehearsals have begun. I've offered to baby-sit. Want her writing career to take off. Easy to play grandma to a delicious child. Thank God had no dinner parties that first week.

All I managed yesterday was to take three pheasants out of the freezer. Half a pheasant each. A simple and tasty dish to prepare.

Looked in my Spanish recipe book hoping to find something Nuria may not have eaten since the days her mother cooked for her. Found nothing. Instead found very good Hungarian prune and walnut strudel recipe. Goes well with coffee. May offer ice cream with it.

Tried to think of a light starter. Nuria, being the lovely lady she is, must be conscious of her figure. Thought of stuffed mushrooms. Those large ones. Instead of usual breadcrumb mixture will serve them topped with fresh prawns.

Thursday
12 September All turned out well. Miss Jackson, we were informed, does not enjoy dinner parties. Did she fear a 'show-biz' evening? Got the feeling Peter imagined he had to tread delicate path. So he neither pressed Glenda to dine nor informed us she probably wouldn't turn up. Can't bear the cowardice of theatre people. As it happens Nuria was relieved not to meet Glenda on same day of arrival. She'd been performing the day before and was whacked.

When A. brought her to front door she exclaimed: 'Dusty, you look wonderful!' 'Except,' I replied, 'I'm fat.' She made a charming stage gesture. Stood in middle of road, put her hands on hips and scowled like a scolding mum. But *she* looks wonderful. Extraordinary for a woman of 55. Handed present of six bottles of 1970 Rioja red. 'For tonight.'

She had a bath, a little sleep. A. to his study, me to remaining preparations. Peter arrived with beautiful bunch of flowers. Robert brought bottle of Glenmorangie whisky. Invited Maite to help with interpreting. She's good but becomes too interested in the conversation. Her interpretation is always behind! Robert discovered he could speak Italian with Nuria, and her English turned out to be adequate. Seems their biggest problem is translation. Nuria has been told by Lorca's sister that Lorca's never been successful in England or America because 'the translations have never got the mixture right of his poetry and theatricality'.

Stuffed Mushrooms with Prawns

12 flat mushrooms, about	1 clove garlic, crushed
3 in / 7 cm across	8 oz / 225 g prawns
2 oz / 50 g melted butter	Salt and pepper to taste
1 tablespoon chopped onion	2 tablespoons chopped parsley

Remove stalks from mushrooms. Place mushrooms on well-buttered flat tin. Chop stalks and cook with onion and seasoning in 1 oz / 25 g butter for about 5 minutes. Remove with slotted spoon and fill the mushroom caps. Place in oven at 190°C / 375°F / gas mark 5 for 15 minutes.

Meanwhile, add remaining butter to pan. Add garlic and cook briefly. Toss in prawns for 3 minutes or so to make hot. When mushrooms are cooked, transfer to serving dish and pile prawns on top of each mushroom. Garnish with parsley.

Pheasant in Sherry Sauce

2 jointed pheasants
2 onions, finely chopped
2 oz / 50 g butter
1 teaspoon ginger
Salt and pepper to taste
1 teaspoon thyme
1 teaspoon parsley

1 teaspoon ground bay leaf
1 teaspoon ground cumin seed
Juice of 1 lemon
1/4 pint / 150 ml sherry
2 tablespoons tomato purée
1/4 pint / 150 ml chicken stock

Using heavy-bottomed ovenproof casserole, cook onions in butter until brown. Add pheasant pieces, ginger, salt and pepper. Fry on low heat for about 20 minutes, turning to brown all sides. Add herbs and spices, lemon juice, sherry, tomato purée and chicken stock. Cover and simmer for 45 minutes until meat is soft. Serve on bed of rice.

Prune and Walnut Strudel

1 lb / 450 g almond pastry
  (see page 109)
8 oz / 225 g walnuts, crushed
1 lb / 450 g prunes, stewed,
  pipped and chopped

2 tablespoons apricot jam
1 egg, beaten

Grease baking sheet.

Mix nuts, prunes and jam. Over a teacloth, roll pastry into very thin rectangle. Spread mixture over entire sheet of pastry. Roll as for apple strudel. (See page 67.) Slip roll on to tin. Brush with beaten egg. Bake at 190°C / 375°F / gas mark 5 for 30 minutes.

Friday   Nuria rang from airport. Very excited. She'd had a 'fantastic'
        13 September   meeting with Glenda Jackson. 'It was women in love . . . she agreed
on the moment, and we all drank champagne.' Pleases me we've
helped an imaginative production on its way.

Now look forward to driving to Brunswick for *Their Very Own And
Golden City*. Need a little adventure.

      Thursday   Impressive production, well received. Ten-minute ovation. Author
      19 September   hauled up on stage to take bow. Never happens on an English stage.

A.'s alarm hadn't worked – somehow knew it wouldn't. Slept
beyond 6 a.m. Leapt out of bed but found had ample time to reach
Dover. Streets empty. Enjoy getting up early, driving through easy
roads. Boat full. Voyage calm. Love ships. If only they didn't have to
move on water! Water terrifies me. My grandfather and an uncle
drowned at sea and my mother handed on a fear of water. Made sure
the fear stopped at me. I can't swim but the children can.

I drove most of the way. A. took over for last two hours. Theatre
chief, Mario Kruger, picked us up in hotel, took us to an Italian
restaurant. Walls full of paintings, atmosphere Bohemian, buzzing
with town's artists. Ate antipasto and 'woolf' fish. New to me.

There's tragedy round every corner. Mario's son was killed in a
cycling accident. His twin sister lived with the pain of it till she was
18, then committed suicide. Broke up his marriage. I'd never survive
such a tragedy but he still communicates. Mario had mounted *The
Golden City* on stage once before in Germany. His favourite. An
admirer of whom we'd not been aware. Thank God someone's out
there rooting for us.

Our German agent, Helmar Fischer, turned up next day. Also our
Turkish friends, Sema and Semra, sisters who live and work in
Berlin. Brunswick mostly destroyed during war. Now has very
modern, attractive centre.

        Sunday   Emotional day. Daniel left to begin new life as a student at the Surrey
        22 September College of Art in Farnham. Drove him there and back yesterday with
his gear so he wouldn't have to haul it on the train. The last of my
children gone. Into the midst of it all came my mother for the day. I
was intensely parent and intensely child packed into a few hours.

Nephew Keith drove her down. He always leaves Norfolk at the
crack of dawn. Was still in dressing gown when they arrived laden

with 40 lb of beans, sack of potatoes, bag of carrots, jars of her home-made pickled onions – all from her garden – six dozen eggs and some of her raspberry jam. Keith went off with his four kids and Janet to the Motor Show, mother stayed behind looking for something to do. Always needs to be useful. No *sitz fleisch*. Decided to string beans, blanch them, put them in the freezer. And the carrots. She not only stringed the beans, she pulled all 40 lb through slicer, then swept the floor and cleaned up after her. Boiling pots of water all over the place. I'd bought some Jewish deli food for her which I know she likes, but she left it behind. Must post it tomorrow. Will the cream cheese survive the mail car? Absolutely exhausted. Bet I fall asleep before my head reaches the pillow.

Magda rang to ask if I'd collect and look after Natasha. Her play previews on Thursday. Can't seem to catch up with housework, but off I rushed.

*Monday
23 September*

Jo reported Daniel in tears as she saw him off at Waterloo Station yesterday. But I spoke to him on phone, he's settling in, making friends. I'm so happy he's going to have a college life.

Sheila Steafel here to rehearse *Yardsale*. A.'s pulled the lounge to pieces to create rehearsal space. Had two weeks of my lounge in a mess when he rehearsed *Annie Wobbler* last year. Can't bear living in that kind of chaos but it saves production costs. Cooked them a mackerel for lunch, with gooseberry sauce.

*Wednesday
25 September*

Mackerel with Gooseberry Sauce

4 medium mackerel	1 tablespoon butter
½ pint / 300 ml water	2 teaspoons sugar
1 tablespoon wine vinegar	½ teaspoon nutmeg
½ lb / 225 g gooseberries	Salt and pepper to taste

Clean mackerel and cut off heads and tails. Lay side by side in ovenproof dish. Add water, vinegar and salt. Cover. Bake at 190°C / 375°F / gas mark 5 for 30 minutes.

Boil gooseberries in 2 tablespoons water. Pass through a sieve into saucepan. Add butter, sugar, salt, pepper and nutmeg. Season carefully, because sauce should have a nice tart taste. Reheat. Pour over mackerel before serving.

Saturday 28 September I'm going to pluck up courage and try to persuade A. to sell this house. He can't bear idea of moving but it's too big for us now. Besides I want a change after 23 years.

Yildiz arrived yesterday from Istanbul to have her pacemaker installed. Sounds like a new washing machine! Daughter, Zeynep, accompanied her to act as nurse during recuperating weeks. Made them a welcome dinner, opened a couple of bottles of champagne, took them to see film *Desperately Seeking Susan*. Pre-operation treat. Fancied cooking something from the past. Borscht. Though God knows why. Not my favourite. Can only drink this soup if taste of beetroot is disguised by taste of beef. Everyone loves it. I'm the only person who doesn't. Wonder why? May stem from childhood days when it was dished up every Sunday afternoon with salad and I was forced to eat it. Father loved it. Used to watch him wide-eyed as he put away mouthfuls covered in vinegar, salt and pepper.

2 lb / 900 g chuck steak, fat
  removed
2 pints / 1.2 litres water
Salt and pepper to taste
1 large onion
½ lb / 225 g white cabbage
4 beetroot
2 carrots

3 sticks celery
1 green pepper
1 dessertspoon vegetable oil
3 bay leaves
6 peppercorns
2 tablespoons tomato purée
¼ pint / 150 ml sour cream
1 tablespoon fresh dill

Cook beef in water seasoned with salt and pepper. Bring to boil, skim and leave to simmer for 2 hours.

Meanwhile dice onion, shred cabbage, slice beet and carrots, chop celery and pepper. Fry onion and green pepper in oil.

Remove beef from liquid. It's the liquid we need. Use meat as you fancy. Add vegetables, fried onion and pepper, bay leaves, peppercorns to broth. Boil for 30 minutes. Add tomato purée. Liquidise.

Serve each plateful with a dollop of sour cream and fresh dill.

Stuffed Trout

4 trout, cleaned and gutted
2 oz / 50 g butter
¼ lb / 100 g green olives,
  chopped
½ large onion, chopped

½ red pepper, chopped
2 oz / 50 g mushrooms, chopped
Salt and pepper to taste
1 oz / 25 g flaked almonds

Butter a rectangular dish.

Cook all ingredients except nuts and trout, for 10 minutes in butter. Stuff cavity of trout with this mixture. Season to taste. Wrap each trout separately in tin foil. Bake in slow oven at 170°C / 327°F / gas mark 3 for 20 minutes. Toast almonds and sprinkle over trout.

Artichokes with Mushrooms and Cheese Sauce

1½ lb / 675 g Jerusalem
  artichokes, boiled and sliced
2 oz / 50 g Cheddar cheese,
  grated
6 oz / 175 g breadcrumbs

4 oz / 100 g mushrooms
2 oz / 50 g butter
2 tablespoons flour
½ pint / 300 ml milk
Salt and pepper to taste

Lay artichokes in buttered, shallow ovenproof dish. Mix grated cheese and breadcrumbs. Cook mushrooms in butter for 5 minutes. Remove with slotted spoon. Stir flour into butter to make roux. Let out with milk. Add salt and pepper to taste. Cover artichokes with mushrooms and pour over sauce. Sprinkle with cheese and breadcrumbs. Bake at 200°C / 400°F / gas mark 6 for 15 minutes.

Pears in Red Wine

6 Conference pears, peeled	Stick of cinnamon
¼ pint / 150 ml red wine	Grated rind of 1 lemon
¼ pint 150 ml water	1 tablespoon arrowroot
4 oz / 100 g castor sugar	2 tablespoons rum

Combine wine, water, sugar, cinnamon and lemon rind in a large saucepan. Bring to boil. Drop in pears. Simmer until tender. Remove pears to serving dish. Thicken juice with arrowroot. Remove from heat. Add rum. Pour over pears. Leave to cool. Serve.

Sunday
29 September
Went for a walk with Yildiz and Zeynep in Kenwood. Fine sunny day. Bumped into friends. Always do in this beautiful park. Will miss it if we have to move far away from the area. Looked in at The Old Kitchen attached to Kenwood House. My dream is one day to organise a function there. Perhaps my 50th birthday next year.

Lisa and John for lunch. She's looking good in fifth month of pregnancy. Started them off with spinach soup which I've always wanted to try my hand at; followed with something else I'd never made before – braised goose. Lisa's always said she's passionate about goose, so wanted to make a fuss of her. Can build up my supply of goose fat for roast potatoes and chopped liver. Goose fat, another childhood memory – of my father spreading it thick on bread.

All of which is filling. To say nothing of the raspberry almond meringue tart I ended with. So didn't give them many vegetables, just sweet and sour red cabbage.

After lunch cab came to take Yildiz to hospital.

Spinach Soup

1 lb / 450 g fresh spinach
1 large onion
Sprig of rosemary
3 oz / 75 g butter
1 tablespoon flour
1 pint / 600 ml chicken stock,
    hot

2 tablespoons breadcrumbs
Salt and pepper to taste
2 egg yolks
¼ pint / 150 ml single cream

Chop spinach and onion. Cook onion and rosemary in butter for 5 minutes. Remove rosemary. Add chopped spinach and sweat for about 10 minutes. Add flour gradually. Let out with hot chicken stock. Stir in breadcrumbs. Season to taste. Simmer for 40 minutes. Leave to cool. Liquidise. Reheat. Beat egg yolks and cream in a tureen and pour on hot soup. Stir well before serving.

Braised Goose

1 goose, 10–12 lb / 4.5–5.5 kg
Salt and pepper to taste
1 lemon
1 lb / 450 g tart apples, peeled
    and sliced
1 lb / 450 g prunes, pitted and
    chopped
¼ pint / 150 ml red wine
½ pint / 300 ml chicken stock
Soya sauce
1 tablespoon arrowroot
2 tablespoons brandy
Redcurrant jelly

Preheat oven at 180°C / 350°F / gas mark 4.

Season goose with salt and pepper. Rub inside with lemon. Mix apple and prunes. Stuff into goose. Secure legs with string. Pour wine into roasting pan. Lay goose on rack in pan. Cook for 4 hours, basting continually. Remove goose to serving plate. Skim all fat off juice. Add chicken stock and soya sauce, thicken with arrowroot and, finally, add brandy.

Serve goose with redcurrant jelly.

Sweet and Sour Red Cabbage

2 lb / 900 g red cabbage,
  shredded

2 medium onions, chopped

1 tablespoon vegetable oil

2 cooking apples, sliced

2 tablespoons brown sugar

¼ pint / 150 ml red wine

2 tablespoons wine vinegar

2 tablespoons chopped fresh
  parsley

1 bay leaf

Salt and pepper to taste

Using heavy-bottomed casserole, cook onion in oil. Add other ingredients. Cover and cook for about 2 hours on low heat.

Raspberry Almond Meringue Tart

1 lb / 450 g almond pastry
  (see page 109)

3 egg whites

6 oz / 175 g castor sugar

6 oz / 175 g ground almonds

1½ lb / 675 g raspberries

4 oz / 100 g toasted almonds

½ pint / 300 ml double cream,
  whipped

Line 10 in / 25 cm flan tin with almond pastry. Bake blind for 15 minutes at 190°C / 375°F / gas mark 5.

Whip egg whites until frothy. Gradually add sugar and fold in ground almonds. Fill pastry shell with fresh raspberries. Spread almond meringue on top. Bake for 30 minutes at 190°C / 375°F / gas mark 5. When cool sprinkle with toasted almonds and serve with whipped cream.

Thursday
3 October   Full days. In the afternoon had to entertain an actor/professor from India. Made a walnut roll.

Wednesday went to preview of Magda's play *God's Second In Command*. Enjoyed it. It's like *Chicken Soup With Barley* without the politics. Many parallels between black and Jewish family life – weak men and strong women, sense of family unity, talk of 'breaking out'. We're bemused by the cycle of things. In the late 50s the Theatre Upstairs used to be a restaurant run by Clement Freud. When *Chicken Soup With Barley* was performed on the main stage in '58, A. and John Dexter, the director, went upstairs to the restaurant to pass time away till early morning reviews appeared. Freud had chicken soup with barley on his menu.

This afternoon the actress, Louise Jameson, came with an actor, David Hodge, to discuss possibility of their mounting a production of *The Four Seasons*. Wanted A.'s permission to let them seek out director and a theatre. Can't understand why that play isn't done more often here. It only needs two characters. Keeps being done around the world.

Early evening memorial service for Michael Haffner in the Church of the Immaculate Conception. About 200 people there. Priest talked of life after death but no one celebrated poor Michael's short life before death.

Went on to see a film called *Dim Sum*. Love this kind of food but found the film dull. Had to walk out half way. Everyone raves about it. Must be one of our blind spots. First-night party next, at Lindsay's flat. Magda, Lindsay, director, cast all turned up in high state of exhilaration. Opening had gone well.

Walnut or Poppy Seed Roll

The pastry

5 oz / 150 g butter
3/4 lb / 350 g flour
1/2 oz / 14 g yeast
1 tablespoon milk

2 tablespoons sour cream
Pinch salt
1 egg, beaten, for glaze

Grease flat baking tray.

Rub butter into flour and put aside. Dissolve yeast in warm milk. Add sour cream and salt. Leave to stand for 15 minutes. Pour liquid into flour and butter mix to form stiff dough. Rest for 30 minutes.

Walnut filling

5 oz / 150 g sugar
2 tablespoons milk
7 oz / 200 g ground walnuts

Rind of 1 lemon, grated
2 tablespoons apricot jam

Using a saucepan, dissolve sugar in milk. Add other ingredients to make paste.

Roll pastry on teacloth as for strudel (see page 67). Spread walnut filling on to pastry. Roll up and slip on to baking tray. Brush with egg. Bake at 180°C / 350°F / gas mark 4 for 40 minutes.

Poppy seed filling

5 oz / 150 g sugar	Rind of 1 lemon, grated
2 tablespoons milk	2 tablespoons apricot jam
6 oz / 175 g ground poppy seed	

Prepare as for walnut filling.

Friday 4 October
Magda rang to inform us of bad review in *The Times*. Billington cool in *The Guardian*, too. Oh my God! In addition to living through nightmares of husband's first nights and subsequent reviews, now have a daughter-in-law's traumas to cope with. Not fair. He wasn't a playwright when I fell for him, just a straightforward kitchen porter living an uncomplicated life in a Norwich hotel!

Yildiz had her pacemaker put in yesterday. Complains it's heavy – maybe it *is* a washing machine. Feels improvement immediately. Her lips are no longer blue. That's today's *good* news.

Today's *bad* news is that the theatre in Israel which bought rights for *Annie Wobbler* has dropped project; and French TV have turned down suggestion to do *The Four Seasons*; A. is leaving his publisher, Jonathan Cape, after 25 years. They've never had a good play list. He stayed only because of his friendship with Tom Maschler. He's just rushed off for a meeting with a possible new publisher, Methuen. Upheaval, upheaval, it's all upheaval!

Meanwhile I've got a houseful of cousins to cook for in two days' time. His, not mine. Been feeling guilty I'd not gathered them together for some time. We'll be about sixteen, including Della, Ralph and my kids. I'm very fond of the cousins, but it's a challenge cooking for them because they're all such fine cooks. In fact, I inherited my favourite cheesecake recipe from one of them. Think I'll cook veal. That's safe. Perhaps with aubergines. And chicken as an alternative. Jews and chicken, can't go wrong. And lots of vegetables. Dessert's the problem with those girls, to find something they may not have tasted before. Or should I go in the opposite direction and give them something they *have* tasted before? Lockshen pudding?

Cousins' gathering went off well. A. got a game of solo going. Like the old days. How I remember the quarrels that used to take place between his mother and the other aunts and uncles over their game of solo. Being a country girl, I could never understand them. Quarrels over cards? What for? They used to frighten me.

Sunday evening to the Mountview Theatre School to see post-graduate students doing their last show, one about Gilbert and Sullivan. A. handed out the diplomas and had to make a speech. Always makes me nervous. Panic he's going to dry up.

Veal with Aubergines

2 lb / 900 g veal, cut in moderate-sized pieces
1 large aubergine, cut into chunks
2 eggs, beaten
2 tablespoons flour
4 teaspoons vegetable oil

2 medium onions, chopped
½ teaspoon paprika
¼ pint / 150 ml water
¼ pint / 150 ml white wine
6 tomatoes, peeled and sliced
Salt and pepper to taste
1 dessertspoon chopped parsley

Salt aubergines. Leave for 30 minutes. Rinse and dry. Dip, chunk by chunk, into beaten eggs, then roll in 1 tablespoon flour. Put aside.

Using heavy-bottomed casserole, fry veal pieces in 2 tablespoons oil until brown. Remove. Fry onions. Add remaining flour and the paprika. Let out with wine and water. Return meat to casserole. Add sliced tomatoes. Cover with lid and simmer until veal is tender. About 45 minutes. If more moisture is needed just add a little water.

Five minutes before veal is ready, fry floured aubergines in remaining oil. Remove with slotted spoon. Drain on kitchen towel.

Serve veal with aubergine pieces as garnish. Decorate with parsley.

Chicken with Walnuts

2 chicken breasts, cut into thin strips
4 oz / 100 g walnuts, chopped
2 tablespoons vegetable oil
1 small onion, chopped
1 stick celery, finely stripped

1 teaspoon sugar
1 dessertspoon arrowroot
2 tablespoons sherry
1 tablespoon soya sauce
¼ pint / 150 ml chicken stock
Salt to taste

Using a wok, stir fry walnuts in hot oil for 3 minutes. Remove nuts and drain on paper towel. Put chicken into wok. Sprinkle with salt. Cook for 5 minutes, stirring. Remove. Next fry onion and celery until tender. Combine sugar, arrowroot, sherry, soya sauce and chicken stock. Pour over vegetables. Stir until sauce starts to thicken. Add walnuts and chicken pieces, to heat through. Serve on bed of rice.

Cabbage with Caraway

2 lb / 900 g white cabbage
1 onion, finely chopped
1 oz / 25 g butter
½ pint / 300 ml chicken stock

1 teaspoon caraway seeds
½ teaspoon salt
Freshly ground pepper

Grate white cabbage. Cook with chopped onion in butter for 10 minutes. Add stock and caraway seeds, and season to taste. Cover and cook for 10 more minutes. Serve hot.

Courgettes with Rosemary

1 lb / 450 g courgettes, sliced
1 medium onion, chopped
1 clove garlic, crushed
2 tablespoons olive oil
1 small tin of tomatoes

2 tablespoons tomato purée
1 sprig fresh rosemary
Salt and pepper to taste
2 tablespoons breadcrumbs
2 tablespoons Parmesan cheese

Fry onion and garlic in olive oil. Add courgettes and cook for 5 minutes. Add tomatoes, tomato purée, rosemary and seasoning. Toss. Turn into ovenproof dish. Mix breadcrumbs with Parmesan and sprinkle on top. Bake at 190°C / 375°F / gas mark 5 for 30 minutes.

Lockshen Pudding

1 lb / 450 g medium noodles,
    boiled
½ pint / 300 ml sour cream
¼ lb / 100 g castor sugar
    (reserve 1 tablespoon)

6 eggs, beaten
¼ lb / 100 g butter, melted
    (reserve 1 tablespoon)
¾ lb / 350 g cream cheese

Butter baking dish, about 12 × 8 in / 30 × 20 cm.
Add sour cream and sugar to beaten eggs. Blend melted butter and cream cheese. Add to cream mixture. Combine with noodles. Pour

into buttered dish. Dot with remaining butter and sprinkle with remaining sugar. Bake at 190°C / 375°F / gas mark 5 for half an hour. Do not allow to become too dry.

Raspberry Sponge

4 oz / 100 g shortcrust pastry	Vanilla essence
12 oz / 350 g raspberries	2 oz / 50 g self-raising flour
2 oz / 50 g butter	1 tablespoon milk
2 oz / 50 g castor sugar	3 oz / 75 g icing sugar
1 egg	

Grease 10 in / 25 cm flan tin.

Roll out pastry and line flan tin. Spread raspberries over pastry.

To make sponge topping, cream butter and castor sugar well. Beat in egg and vanilla. Fold in the flour. Add milk to obtain soft consistency. Spread mixture over raspberries. Bake in centre of oven at 190°C / 375°F / gas mark 5 for about 35 minutes or until sponge is springy. Dredge with icing sugar and serve hot.

Went last night to see *Torch Song Trilogy*. Enjoyed it. Six of us. Della, Ralph and Israeli friends David and Rachel Tené. Della brought sad news that Uncle Layosh in Roumania is dead. The last of Mother Wesker's brothers. And this morning attended stone-setting for Aunty Betty and Uncle Perly. Perly was the one-before-last of her brothers. The wealthy side of A.'s family. And generous with it. No more aunts and uncles left on his mother's side – either in England, Roumania or Israel. End of an era for them, I suppose.

Sunday
13 October

Letter from Daniel. Writes that his fellow students all agreed I should live with them for a month as their provider and cook!

House overflowing. Lindsay's having central heating installed in his flat. He, Magda and baby, plus Tanya, plus two Turks. Then out of the blue Henryk (Bering-Llisberg) rang to ask could he stay the night on his way from New York to Copenhagen (where he runs the Royal Theatre). Had to put mattress on lounge floor for him. Love it when house is full of my family.

Cooked something very special – pheasant with apple. And had to use up raspberries. Made a raspberry cream and an apple pudding. Lots of vegetables, of course.

Pheasant with Apple and Bread Sauce

1 pheasant, jointed	Salt and pepper to taste
4 oz / 100 g bacon, diced	2 large cooking apples
1 medium onion, chopped	½ pint / 300 ml chicken stock
1 clove garlic, chopped	1 tablespoon Cointreau
2 oz / 50 g butter	½ pint / 300 ml single cream

Using heavy-bottomed casserole, fry bacon, onion and garlic in butter. Remove with slotted spoon. Put aside. Brown jointed pheasant in remaining butter. Season to taste. Remove pheasant. Fry sliced apple. Return bacon, onion and pheasant to casserole. Add chicken stock. Cover and simmer for 40 minutes. Remove from heat. Stir in cream and Cointreau.

Bread sauce

¾ pint / 400 ml milk	8 tablespoons white
Pinch mace	breadcrumbs
6 peppercorns, crushed	Salt and pepper to taste
1 medium onion	1 teaspoon butter
4 cloves	2 tablespoons cream

In a saucepan, stir mace and peppercorns into milk. Push cloves into onion. Add to milk. Bring to boil. Put aside to infuse for 30 minutes. Strain milk into another saucepan. Add breadcrumbs and stir until boiling and thick. Season to taste. Remove from heat. Stir in butter and cream. Serve alongside pheasant.

Leeks Braised in White Wine

10 leeks	¼ pint / 150 ml water
¼ lb / 100 g bacon, diced	Salt and pepper to taste
¼ pint / 150 ml white wine	

Wash leeks very, very carefully. Halve them. Place in casserole with diced bacon. Season well. Add wine and water. Cover and braise at 180°C / 350°F / gas mark 4 for 1 hour.

Sweetcorn Fritters

4 oz / 100 g sweetcorn kernels	½ teaspoon baking powder
4 oz / 100 g breadcrumbs	Salt and pepper to taste
2 eggs	Oil for frying

Mix ingredients. Form into small cakes. Fry in a little hot oil until brown.

Raspberry Cream

1 lb / 450 g raspberries, frozen	4 tablespoons sugar
Juice of 1 lemon	3 egg yolks
1 oz / 25 g gelatine	¾ pint / 400 ml double cream

Defrost raspberries in lemon juice. Strain. Heat raspberry juice to dissolve gelatine. Push raspberries through sieve to remove seeds. Put juice in blender. Gradually add sugar, sieved raspberries and egg yolks. Blend for 1 minute. Add double cream and blend until smooth. Pour into blancmange mould. Chill until set.

Apple and Rice Pudding

4 oz / 100 g long grain rice	2 tablespoons apricot jam
1 pint / 600 ml milk	1 lb / 450 g Cox's apples, cooked
4 tablespoons castor sugar	1 egg
¼ pint / 150 ml double cream	4 tablespoons ground almonds

Cook rice in saucepan with milk and 2 tablespoons sugar. Don't let it get too mushy. Remove from heat and allow to cool. Whip cream slightly and add to rice.

Spread layer of apricot jam in bottom of an ovenproof dish. Put in alternate layers of cooked apples and creamed rice until dish is almost full. Whip egg and remaining sugar. Fold in ground almonds. Spread over top. Bake at 190°C / 375°F / gas mark 5 for 35 minutes. Serve hot.

Lorraine, my niece from Norfolk, here these last few days. Daughter *Wednesday* of my sister who died of leukemia last year. Very much looked *23 October* forward to having her with me. Bright girl. Says she's thinking of going into banking. Her first time in London. In fact she's hardly been outside Norfolk. Been showing her shops and sights. But today was the big day. Drove to Stratford-on-Avon to see Sheila in *Yardsale*. Three performances as part of the RSC actors' festival. Only a half-hour piece but one of my favourites. I'd promised to bring up a lunch basket for everyone but was too busy. Wanted day off, besides. Lorraine thrilled.

She's going with Tanya to see *Les Misérables* tomorrow night. We saw it last week. A. kept finishing the rhymes of the songs before they happened. But I enjoyed it.

Saturday
26 October

The Merchant had German première in Augsburg last Sunday. Telegram from them claimed first night was great success. Helmar rang to say it was success with audience. Grateful to get their teeth into a text with substance, he said, instead of watching a director's high jinks across the stage. But 'critics sat on the fence'.

Still find each day nerve-wracking, even after all these years. News good and news bad keeps coming at us: at the breakfast table when the mail's opened; in phone calls which I have to intercept during the day; when A. returns from meetings. That damn wheel of fortune occupies my mind constantly. The National Theatre of Northern Greece have applied to do *The Kitchen*. A theatre in Lyons wants to present *Annie Wobbler* and take it to Paris. A non-profit-making troupe in NY want to do what they call 'a major off-off Broadway production of *The Journalists*'. How can anything off-off Broadway be major?! Our agent reports a good meeting with Peter Mayer of Penguin Books. Like Methuen, they're interested in taking on A. as an original author. All 'maybes'. Maybe, maybe. So tired of 'maybes'. I want a big generous 'yes' from someone.

Gunther Klotz from East Berlin wants to discuss long essay he plans, comparing *The Journalists* to the Hare/Brenton play *Pravda*. Lunch the only time he was free. Had to concoct something quickly. Decided I'd try stuffed pancakes.

Following Gunther at 4 p.m. – the time A. meets people in the hope a day's work might be done by then – there came a pretty Italian student to talk about her thesis on *The Four Seasons*. He's stopped seeing thesis writers. Says they ask questions they should be answering for themselves, but this thesis sounded original. Baked her cinnamon balls.

6 pre-made crêpes · 1 egg, hard-boiled and grated
  (see page 57) · Generous pinch nutmeg
½ lb / 225 g spinach, cooked

Cheese sauce

2 oz / 50 g butter · 2 oz / 50 g Cheddar cheese,
1 tablespoon flour · grated
½ pint / 300 ml milk · Salt and pepper to taste

Melt butter. Add flour to make roux. Let out with milk. Stir in cheese. Season. Mix spinach with the cheese sauce. Add nutmeg. Mix in grated hard-boiled egg. Spread on pancakes and roll up. Lay filled pancakes in rectangular oven dish. Cover and cook at 190°C / 375°F / gas mark 5 for 15 minutes.

Cinnamon Balls

2 egg whites · 1 teaspoon cinnamon
4 oz / 100 g castor sugar · 1 oz / 25 g icing sugar
4 oz / 100 g ground almonds

Grease baking sheet.

Whip egg whites until stiff. Fold in sugar, ground almonds and cinnamon. Roll into walnut-size balls. Lay on baking sheet. Bake at 170°C / 325°F / gas mark 3 for 20 minutes. When cool roll in icing sugar.

Michael Holroyd's 50th Saturday evening. Lots of old friends there. *Monday* Some enemies, too. But pretended they didn't exist. Noisy. Everyone *28 October* shouting to be heard. Nice to be fed, though.

What am I going to do for *my* 50th? Told everyone very firmly I don't want a fuss. No surprise party, no hordes of friends and relatives cooking for me, and it's for sure *I* don't want to cook and clear up. On the other hand, I want *something* to happen. A. suggested alternatives: a long week-end in Paris with the children, stay with friends, eat in our favourite restaurants; dinner with the children in somewhere like Le Caprice with a cruise to the sun as dessert; fifty of my favourite people for a meal in Lauderdale House in Highgate with the Travelling Gourmets to cater for it. 'How do we pay for it?' I asked. Told me not to worry, we'd find the money somewhere. Which is how we've always lived and planned. I suggested we could afford it if we sold the house! Don't know what I want. Have to decide soon.

Eric Standidge who directed *Yardsale* for Edinburgh Fringe came for tea and stayed to share our dinner. Thank God I do cook too much, as the children often complain I do.

Family for Sunday lunch yesterday, including Daniel who's having problems of the heart. Drove him back to Farnham. A. wanted to see the college and his room. Tanya came for the ride. Nice crowd of kids around him. Shares a tiny room with a tall fellow. Six others along the passage share a kitchen. Left him a supply of food which goes into the kitty.

Sunday lunch was an experiment. Thought I'd try out stuffed shoulder of lamb. Lamb is another of my passions. Can never have enough of it. Problem was I needed two to feed so many. Should only experiment on a small scale. My kids love crêpes. Made them crêpes. With Grand Marnier sauce.

Elsa rang from Copenhagen to announce not only was Ole coming for three weeks to do research but she was joining him in the last week. Exit the Turks, enter the Danes. Love my friends, though. A. wrote a story about a holiday we had together with the Danes when Ole was doing research in Cambridge. 'The Visit', a long, loving work. Not my favourite, however.

Stuffed Shoulder of Lamb

2 boned shoulders of lamb
¼ pint / 150 ml white wine

Stuffing

1 pint / 600 ml stock made from
   lamb bones
2 oz / 50 g butter
1 tablespoon mixed herbs
1 medium onion, finely
   chopped

4 oz / 100 g mushrooms,
   chopped
4 oz / 100 g fresh breadcrumbs
3 oz / 75 g cooked ham, chopped
3 oz / 75 g veal mince
Salt and pepper to taste

Fry onions and mushrooms in butter. In a bowl assemble all other ingredients except wine. Mix well. Add onions and mushrooms. Open out the shoulder of lamb and spread with stuffing. Roll and tie securely. Place in roasting tin. Pour over wine. Cook at 200°C / 400°F / gas mark 6 for 1½ hours.

Vegetable Pilau

1 lb / 450 g carrots
1 small cauliflower
8 oz / 225 g leeks
2 oz / 50 g butter
1 green pepper, chopped
12 oz / 350 g long grain rice
1 level teaspoon ground
   cardamom

1 level teaspoon ground paprika
½ teaspoon ground cloves
½ teaspoon ground cinnamon
1¾ pints / 1 litre chicken stock
Salt and pepper to taste
1 tablespoon chopped parsley

Peel and slice carrots thinly. Divide cauliflower into small florets. Cut leeks in ½ in / 1.2 cm slices. Using ovenproof casserole, melt butter and fry carrots, cauliflower, leeks and green pepper until nicely brown, about 5 minutes. Stir in rice and spices. Cook for 1 minute, stirring. Pour in stock. Season well. Bring to boil. Cover casserole, and cook for 15 minutes on medium heat. Garnish with parsley.

Crêpes in Grand Marnier

Make 12 crêpes (see page 57).

Grand Marnier sauce

4 oz / 100 g butter	Juice of 2 oranges
4 oz / 100 g castor sugar	1 tablespoon brandy
Rind of 1 orange, grated	3 tablespoons Grand Marnier

In a saucepan melt butter, then add sugar, orange rind, and juice. Heat until sugar dissolves into syrupy sauce. Mix in brandy and Grand Marnier. Ignite, pour over crêpes, and serve flaming.

Friday
1 November

Ole's settled in as though he's always lived here. Claims he's become more introvert while Elsa's become more extrovert.

Sloane Bosniak came to town, a New York actress who bought US rights for *Annie Wobbler*. Met her on my New York trip. Couldn't remember if she's a health food freak. A. arranged to pick her up for lunch with Pamela so she could see Pam's designs for the play. Wednesday last she came to lunch before A. took her to Cambridge to hear his lecture on *The Merchant*. Made scallops, easy and light. And a dessert that sounded American, blueberry pie. Today she joined 18 Norwegian drama students who came to Bishops Road to hear A. read from and talk about *Annie*. Baked them a tea of three different cakes and some interestingly filled *vols au vents*.

Monday last went to first night of Magda's second play *Basin*. Took Ole. All enjoyed it. Magda and L.J. upset because director and cast had cut without asking her. 'They cut what they couldn't handle.' How often have I heard A. say that. L.J. objected to use of Bach as interval music. The director, a black woman, had argued: 'Why should it always be that loud reggae music for a black play?' L.J. thinks her view patronising. 'It says: "Look, we blacks can be cultured when we like."'

Went to Stoppard revival of his play *The Real Inspector Hound*. Part of a double bill with Sheridan's *The Critic*. Martyn Naylor, our Japanese agent, arranged the tickets. Two Japanese actors and their hostess with us. Enjoyed it. Kept looking at Japanese to see what they were making of it. They were struggling. Not many smiles. Hostess an exquisite Japanese lady, a music-lover, who supports Japanese musicians. Married to a business man who buys and sells things like tanks and submarines. Meet all sorts married to a playwright! Ate in Joe Allen's afterwards. One of my favourite eating places. High-class junk food.

A. got a call from his agent, Nat. 'You sitting down?' he asked. 'Good news or bad?' A. asked. Turned out to be good. A plan for production of *The Merchant*. To open at the Leeds Playhouse, move down to the Old Vic for six weeks. I'll believe it when I see it.

Yesterday lunch with Swedish Ambassador and his wife, to meet a visiting group of Swedish actors. Among the guests was the Bergman actor Max von Sydow. He's so tall. Always admired him. In the evening to Christie's for launching of the British Israel Arts Trust, a kind of Israeli 'British Council'. A.'s brainchild which others had put into practice. Met Leila and Dave Lee, the composer. Hadn't seen them for ages. That was a good musical he'd written with A. all those years ago, *Stand Up! Stand Up!* Commissioned by Jack Hylton who loved the music but found the lyrics 'too depressing'. Pity. I can still sing the melodies.

Funny encounter at the launching. Met a man who said: 'Oh, I'm only a shop-keeper, and I wanted my son to be what I couldn't be.' A. said it depended what the shop was called. 'If it's called Marks and Spencer . . .' 'No,' said the man, 'it's called Debenhams and Hamleys and Harvey Nichols . . .'

Must think about making my Christmas puddings before we leave for Montreal.

Scallops and Jerusalem Artichokes

4 scallops	Sprig of parsley
¼ pint / 150 ml white wine	4 large Jerusalem artichokes,
¼ pint / 150 ml water	finely sliced
Bay leaf	¼ pint / 150 ml milk
6 peppercorns	

Simmer scallops with wine, water, peppercorns, bay leaf and parsley for 10 minutes.

Cook artichokes in milk until tender.

1 oz / 25 g butter	1 tablespoon flour
1 medium onion, finely chopped	¼ pint / 150 ml single cream
	4 tablespoons breadcrumbs
4 oz / 100 g button mushrooms	Salt and pepper to taste

Melt butter and fry onion. Add chopped mushrooms. Cook for 5 minutes. Remove onion and mushrooms with slotted spoon. Set aside. Sift flour into butter and make a roux. Let out with scallop stock, cream and artichoke juice until smooth sauce. Add onions and mushrooms. Put scallops and artichokes into scallop shells. Cover with sauce. Sprinkle with breadcrumbs. Dot with butter. Bake at 180°C / 350°F / gas mark 4 for 10 minutes.

Blueberry Pie

½ lb / 225 g shortcrust pastry	1 tablespoon arrowroot
2 lb / 900 g blueberries, fresh	2 eggs, separated
¼ pint / 150 ml water	1 small carton sour cream
6 oz / 175 g sugar	

Grease 10 in / 25 cm pie tin. Line with shortcrust pastry.

Cook blueberries in water until soft, about 5 minutes. Add sugar and arrowroot. Allow to cool. Spoon blueberry mix over pastry. Blend sour cream and eggs. Pour over fruit. Bake at 190°C / 375°F / gas mark 5 for 40 minutes.

This can be made with pastry on top, too.

Marble Cake

6 eggs, separated	2 teaspoons vanilla
8 oz / 225 g sugar	12 oz / 350 g self-raising flour
¼ pint / 150 ml vegetable oil	2 tablespoons cocoa
¾ pint / 400 ml orange juice	

Grease 8 in / 20 cm cake tin.

Beat egg whites until stiff. Fold in sugar. Beat egg yolks with oil, orange juice and vanilla. Mix in cocoa and flour. Fold in egg whites to create a marbled effect. (The more you mix, the less marbled the effect.) Pour into tin. Bake at 190°C / 375°F / gas mark 5 for about 1 hour or until firm to touch. Leave to cool in tin.

Banana Sponge Cake

8 large eggs, separated
6 oz / 175 g sugar
Rind of 1 lemon, grated
Juice of ½ lemon
1 large banana, mashed
3 oz / 75 g self-raising flour

Pinch of salt
1 tablespoon arrowroot
2 oz / 50 g walnuts, finely
    chopped

Grease 10 in / 25 cm loose-bottomed cake tin.

Beat egg yolks until light. Add sugar and continue beating. Mix in lemon rind and juice and mashed banana. Sift flour, salt and arrowroot. Fold into egg mix. Fold in nuts. Whip whites until stiff. fold into cake mix. Bake at 180°C / 350°F / gas mark 4 for 1 hour.

Curd Cake

8 oz / 225g shortcrust pastry
1 lb / 450 g curd cheese
2 oz / 50 g butter
4 tablespoons castor sugar
2 eggs

1 teaspoon cinnamon
2 tablespoons brandy
2 tablespoons double cream
2 oz / 50 g sultanas, washed

Line a deep 10 in / 25 cm pie tin with shortcrust pastry. Bake blind.

Using blender, combine cheese, butter, sugar, eggs, cinnamon, brandy and cream. Lay sultanas on pastry base. Pour cheese mixture on top. Bake at 180°C / 350°F / gas mark 4 for 30 minutes.

Leave for Canada in six days to see *The Kitchen* so today was Xmas Pudding Day.

*Monday
4 November*

For years A. has been trying to persuade me to go into business making vintage Christmas puddings. But each pudding has to boil for nine hours! (The longer you boil the blacker it becomes, and I like mine very black.) I'd go mad! Too much else to think about. Takes me all my time to make five! Give one each to people who haven't the patience to steam their own. Such as Mikki, A.'s ex-secretary and one of our oldest friends. Also good as presents for dinner parties instead of the usual bottle of wine or box of chocolates.

Can't pretend I make cheap ole things. (A. complains my extravagance keeps us in overdraft.) I'm very lavish with brandy, rum and stout in which I soak all the dried fruit overnight. Based on a recipe which Mrs Thomas Hardy baked for her husband. A. keeps vowing to write a novel. Might help. Who knows?

Reviews of Magda's play good except for a stupid one by Nicholas de Jong. Relief throughout the family.

Also relieved to see L.J., Magda and babe out of here and back in their flat. Never thought I'd be so glad to see my darling Natasha go, but age is telling. The house has been so cluttered. Trip to Canada will be very welcome.

A. came down waving a letter in utter amazement. From an Indian doing a post-graduate thesis on his work. Requested we send him all the books and plays without offering to pay!

Christmas Pudding

1 lb / 450 g raisins	10 oz / 275 g brown sugar
10 oz / 275 g sultanas	1/4 teaspoon salt
1 lb / 450 g currants	Rind of 2 lemons, grated
1/4 pint / 150 ml rum	5 oz / 150 g candied peel
1/4 pint / 150 ml sherry	3 oz / 75 g chopped almonds
10 oz / 275 g shredded suet	2 large cooking apples, peeled,
10 oz / 275 g breadcrumbs	cored and grated
8 oz / 225 g self-raising flour	8 eggs
2 teaspoons mixed spice	1 can stout
1 teaspoon nutmeg	Juice of 2 lemons

Grease five 1 lb / 450 g pudding basins. Have ready greaseproof paper, teacloths, tin foil and string.

Soak raisins, sultanas and currants in rum and sherry overnight.

In a large mixing bowl rub together suet, breadcrumbs, flour, mixed spice, nutmeg, sugar and salt. Add lemon rind, candied peel, almonds and apples. Mix well. Add currants, raisins, sultanas and rum to mixture. Beat eggs. Add to mixture. Finally stir in stout and lemon juice. Let everyone have a stir.

Spoon mixture into greased basins. Cover with greaseproof paper, then tin foil. Tie down teacloths. Steam for 8 hours.

To store, replace wet paper, foil and cloth with fresh. On the day you wish to eat puddings, steam for a further 2 hours. Serve flaming with brandy and with vanilla cream.

Loved Montreal trip, though not a city I'd want to live in. Saw my first snow. What's winter without snow, I say. Did a lot of eating out, walking and listening to A. answer stupid questions from journalists who knew little or nothing about him. He gave a lecture set up by the drama department of McGill University. Small audience and not one drama student. Want to run away on those occasions.

Sunday 17 November

Our Canadian agent, Muriel Gold, opened her flat and invited theatre people to hear A. give reading of *Annie Wobbler*. Full house. He reads well. May have done some good. Spent a day in their cottage in the Laurentians. Saw run-through of *La Cuisine*, on set in the workshop. Cast nervous, but we soon developed a relationship with them. It looks good. I took a shine to the director, Guillermo de Andrea, a little man from Argentina with laughing eyes. He'd directed *The Kitchen* eight years ago for his theatre in Quebec. Couldn't stay for first night as A. had commitments in London. I left money for a cake from us to be decorated for their first-night party.

After run-through went with director, theatre chief and translator to an Italian restaurant. As the clock struck midnight I raised my glass to A. and wished him happy wedding anniversary. It was our 27th.

Went last evening to buffet given for 'special clients' by our bank in Finsbury Park. One other 'special client' was a young detective inspector. Had a go at him about the treatment of the black community. Surprised myself. Wonderful what you can say, tanked up with a couple of glasses of wine. He conceded things could be better. Told our bank manager he should have paid me to do the catering. He'd have got better than ham sandwiches.

Wednesday 20 November

A. invited to deliver paper to bi-annual conference of International Theatre Critics in Rome. That should be an interesting confrontation! Warned him to keep his nose clean. We've suffered enough from his replies to critics. I'm amazed at his naivety sometimes. He can't understand why critics can't take criticism!

Eight days since last entry. Cooked dinner for family last night. Nothing special. Della and Ralph dropped in unexpectedly. Special lunch today, however, for Nat and Dieter Meichsner who flew in from Hamburg. Dieter is head of drama for Norddeutscher Rundfunk. Eighteen months ago he'd commissioned A. to write four 90-minute plays based on Arthur Koestler's novel *Thieves In The Night*. A. very keen because setting was Palestine in the 1930s. He'd made two trips to Israel for research, had written the four plays twice over. A French film director became involved. They worked for three days on second draft to produce notes for a third draft. (I cooked them endless meals.) Director finally took scripts into his own hands and made a soap opera of them.

Fortunately Dieter didn't want a soap opera. He'd dismissed the French director – who'd behaved presumptuously – abandoned ideas of an international co-production, 'too impossible to achieve', and now wanted Nat to make a last attempt to set up co-production just with a British company. If that couldn't happen, he said, he'd have to commission a new script in German and go it alone for a purely German audience. A. has worked hard and we were banking on the venture for future income. That's why I never believe anything until I see it.

Cooked them something special for good luck; artichoke soufflé. Not made it before. Took a salmon trout out of freezer. Put it together with baked courgettes, normally with me a simple steamed or sautéed vegetable. But in 1978, holidaying in a cabin by a lake in Maine, I discovered baked zucchini. An unusual accompaniment for trout. Peach pie for dessert.

The visit to Maine was one of the most memorable times in my life. (A. was rehearsing *The Merchant* for Broadway.) Such lovely noises in the night. Can still hear them. Was alone with the kids in a marvellous community of Ashkenazy Jewish women and their families from Great Neck, Huntingdon and New York. They'd bought these tiny ex-army cabins for their annual holidays. Someone should make a movie of their years – friendships, deaths, separations, children growing up . . . Every year, at the end of the harvest, there was a gigantic feast. Each cabin dweller cooked something. This particular recipe came from a woman in the next cabin of whom I became very fond, Gloria Osborne. She died two years later of cancer. My contribution to the feast was a trifle. Bought the biggest bowl I could find. They'd never seen anything like it. It's been made every year since.

Artichoke Soufflé

1½ lb / 675 g Jerusalem
   artichokes, peeled
1 pint / 600 ml milk
2 eggs, separated
2 oz / 50 g plain flour

Salt and pepper to taste
1 oz / 25 g Cheddar cheese,
   grated
1 oz / 25 g butter

Grease 8 in / 20 cm soufflé dish.

   Boil artichokes in milk. Strain when soft. Retain some of the liquid. Blend artichokes and egg yolks, adding enough liquid to make loose mixture. Fold in flour and stiffly whipped egg whites. Season to taste. Pour into soufflé dish and sprinkle on cheese. Dot with butter. Bake at 230°C / 450°F / gas mark 8 for 20 minutes.

Salmon Trout with Watercress Sauce

5 lb / 2.2 kg salmon trout
2 oz / 50 g butter

Salt and pepper to taste

Put butter and seasoning into cavity of the fish. Wrap in tin foil and place on baking tray. Bake at 180°C / 350°F / gas mark 4 for 50 minutes, when skin should come away easily with tip of knife. Retain juice.

Watercress sauce

Bunch of watercress
1 fish stock cube
½ pint / 300 ml water
1 oz / 25 g butter

1 tablespoon flour
Salt and pepper to taste
2 tablespoons cream

Cut leaves of watercress from stalks with sharp scissors.

   Dissolve fish stock cube in water. Add fish juice. Simmer stalks of watercress in fish stock for half an hour. Strain. Retain liquid. Using another saucepan, melt butter. Add flour to make roux. Let out with warm stock. Season to taste. Stir in cream and watercress leaves.

   Pour over trout or serve on the side.

Baked Courgettes

3 lb / 1.3 kg courgettes	3 eggs, beaten
1 large onion, grated	3 oz / 75 g mild Cheddar cheese,
2 lb / 900 g parsley	grated
3 tablespoons matzo meal	2 oz / 50 g butter
Salt and pepper to taste	1 teaspoon paprika

Grease deep rectangular baking dish.

Cut off ends of courgettes. Wash but do not peel.

Grate courgettes into a bowl. Add onion, parsley, matzo meal, salt, pepper and eggs. Mix well. Pour mixture into baking dish. Sprinkle with cheese. Dot with butter. Sprinkle with paprika. Bake uncovered at 170°C / 325°F / gas mark 3 for 40 minutes.

Peach Pie

1 lb / 450 g shortcrust pastry	1 teaspoon cinnamon
6 peaches, peeled,	2 egg yolks
pitted and halved	½ pint / 300 ml double cream
4 oz / 100 g brown sugar	

Line 9 in / 22 cm pie tin with shortcrust pastry.

Lay peach halves in pastry shell. Mix sugar and cinnamon and sprinkle over peaches. Bake at 180°C / 350°F / gas mark 4 for 15 minutes. Beat together yolks and cream. Pour over cooked peaches. Bake for further 30 minutes until brown.

Friday
29 November May not have done much *special* cooking, but don't stop *thinking* about cooking in my own chaotic fashion. Shouldn't be compiling a cook book really. Never know what I'm going to cook till I'm out looking. Go into Waitrose, walk to the fish counter, look, walk to the meats, back to the fish counter, wander off to look at something else, then back to the fish counter. And each time the man asks: 'Can I help you, madam?' and I say: 'No, just looking.' I contemplate something with scallops and end up with duck! I see a jar of capers and say to myself: I like capers, must cook something with capers. Or a bag of button mushrooms looks so attractive I buy them whether I want them or not. Sometimes feel I never want to cook another thing in my whole life; next second a jar of cherries sets me off imagining all the things I might do with them. I understand why women buy frozen

meals. Seven main meals a week, 52 weeks a year, times 27 (if you can last as long as I have) equals 9828 meals, minus the times you've eaten or been invited out. That's a lot of thinking and planning.

Been talking to A. about selling the house. Here and there, now and then. Point out he won't have overdraft to worry about, that there'd be spare cash to make changes to the Welsh cottage which he's always wanted to do. Says we've lived with bank overdraft most of our life, he's used to it. Always had this faith that someone somewhere sooner or later will do a play, royalties would keep coming. He's been right so far, but I find it gets more and more hair-raising.

Persuaded him to look at houses on offer in the market. Viewed a mansion flat nearby in Wood Lane. Better than either of us anticipated: two large rooms, small kitchen, a master bedroom, two smaller ones. A. hardly said anything. Just stood around in gloomy silence. For newly-weds, he said finally. I'm going to have a hard time shifting him out of this house. On the other hand don't think I could live anywhere without a garden, or a large kitchen come to that.

Must think what I'm going to cook for Jiri Mucha tomorrow. *There's* an interesting story. How long have we known him? Son of painter Alphonse Mucha. He translated *The Kitchen* into Czech. I saw the Prague production in 1962. (A. couldn't make it.) When art nouveau, and his father's work in particular, was revived all over the world, Jiri travelled from capital to capital ensuring royalties were paid for the posters, writing paper, postcards and the surge of new books on the period. Lives in a fantastic castle, in the middle of Prague, full of his father's paintings. Took the children there in 1973. They stared wide-eyed at figures in armour, winding staircases, oak-panelled rooms, the cobwebs. Said Tanya: 'It's the kind of place where they make horror movies.' Said Lindsay Joe: 'It's the kind of place where they have orgies.'

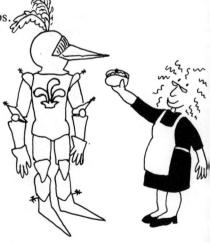

Invited Richard and Maria to meet him. A novelist from Prague to meet one from Montreal and one from Lisbon. Think I'll try stuffed cabbage rolls in tomato sauce, with creamed carrots. And an apple pie.

Monday
2 December
Jiri had flu. Rang in the morning to cancel lunch. Richard and Maria had it to themselves. Well, not quite. There was Tanya, L.J., Magda, us.

Richard brought Part Two of his three-part novel *Italia Perversa* and news of a good review in the *Times Lit. Supp*. Maria brought news that her new novel had just been bought by a French publisher. Three cheers for good news brought by friends 'cos there's none in the newspapers. Can't get recent P L O hi-jackings out of my head. In Malta. They shot a passenger every hour. Among them two young Israeli women. They shot one and threw her on the tarmac where she acted dead but survived. Then they called for the other, who refused to identify herself. They walked down the aisle checking faces with her passport photograph, found her, dragged her screaming down the aisle to the door and shot her. I think of her terror in those moments of them walking down the aisle and I hate the human race.

But still have to cook for them. Our German agents for lunch tomorrow.

Stuffed Cabbage Rolls in Tomato Sauce

1 large white cabbage

Remove as much of stalk from cabbage as possible. Place in large saucepan. Cover with water, add salt and, with lid on, bring to boil. Simmer until leaves are pliable. Remove from saucepan and peel off leaves very carefully. Set aside.

Stuffing

4 oz / 100 g cooked rice	1/4 pint / 150 ml single cream
1 tablespoon breadcrumbs	2 oz / 50 g butter
8 oz / 225 g minced beef, uncooked	Salt and pepper to taste

Grease large ovenproof dish with the butter. Mix rice, breadcrumbs, minced meat and cream. Spread out each cabbage leaf. Put about a tablespoon of stuffing into centre. Roll to form small parcels. Lay side by side in ovenproof dish. Season to taste.

Tomato sauce

½ lb / 225 g ripe tomatoes	1 tablespoon tomato purée
2 tablespoons olive oil	1 teaspoon oregano
1 large onion, finely chopped	Salt and freshly ground black
2 cloves garlic, crushed	pepper to taste
Juice of 1 lemon	

Peel tomatoes by dropping them into boiling water. Skin will come off easily. Chop flesh. Using a saucepan, heat olive oil and fry onion and garlic for 5 minutes. Add tomato flesh, lemon juice, tomato purée, oregano and seasoning. Bring to boil, then simmer for 20 minutes.

Cover cabbage rolls with sauce. Bake at 190°C / 375°F / gas mark 5 for 1 hour.

Creamed Carrots

1 lb / 450 g carrots, cut into	1 tablespoon chopped parsley
pieces	Salt and ground black pepper
¼ pint / 150 ml single cream	to taste
½ oz / 14 g butter	

Cook carrots in salted water for 30 minutes. Drain and mash. Melt butter. Add cream. Pour over carrots. Add black pepper to taste. Sprinkle parsley as garnish before serving.

Apple Orange Pie

1 lb / 450 g shortcrust pastry	Grated rind of 2 oranges
2 lb / 900 g cooking apples	¼ pint / 150 ml water
peeled, cored and sliced	1 egg yolk
2 tablespoons dark brown sugar	

Line 10 in / 25 cm pie tin with half the pastry.

Stew apples with sugar and orange rind in water for 15 minutes. Leave to cool, then pile into pastry shell. Cover with remaining pastry. Brush with egg yolk. Bake at 200°C / 400°F / gas mark 6 for 45 minutes.

In Wales to close up cottage for winter. Worry more about this place than A. does, even though I like it less. Feel ashamed to have little feeling for such a beautiful spot. The sea, the sea, I long for the sea. To wake up in the morning and see a huge ocean. A. can spend weeks here alone writing his plays and stories. The rooms hold special memories for him. Me, I get restless after 48 hours.

But I do love sitting in front of the log fire. And it *is* possible to read here. So quiet. Can think in peace about cooking for Christmas which is upon us. Always a busy time for me.

Made my Christmas puddings in early November with plenty of spirits. Seven weeks to 'mature'. Suppose A. was right. Xmas puddings *could* be a good little cottage industry. For someone. Just not me. Must think about my cake. Won't contemplate those sugar sweets or the game pies some people make for Xmas. I know it's a slice of Old England but it adds the dreaded pounds. Look who's talking!

What huge Christmas parties I *used* to make! For as many as 80 friends and family. Tables groaned with a variety of dishes. Now I make only little supper parties for my favourite people. Put them in the season's mood. For ten consecutive years the high point of a party was the lucky dip. During the year we'd buy odd bits of china, or glass, or interesting knick-knacks, wrap them up individually, lower them into a large bed cover and haul it downstairs into midst of throng. Women had first dip, then male friends, then male family, last were the children – *their* big day was Christmas morning. In the beginning everything we bought had to be no more than 25p. Crept up to 50p. Last years had to spend 75p. Those were the good ole times. I was younger. And beautiful little pieces of glass and china could be had for next to nothing.

But still need to make Xmas a very special occasion. That's what my family like. The best-loved time is Christmas morning. My one luxury of the year is to have champagne and smoked salmon sandwiches for breakfast as we sit around the fire and open gifts. Friends drop in to share the champagne while their own turkey is roasting. This year will be special. We'll have Natasha.

Week before Christmas I'll make my own mincemeat and mince pies. Stick them in the freezer. Won't have job of rolling pastry on that hectic day.

For past eight years have always cooked turkey for the Jackson's

Lane Community Centre. They provide Christmas lunch for local old-age pensioners. A. would transport it, along with roast potatoes, gravy and stuffing, and join line of men who carved. Think this year I'll give another, younger woman in Highgate the opportunity to be blessed.

From childhood can remember how my mum, with the little she had, made Christmas a special occasion for us kids. Presents were very important. I try to continue in her footsteps. My family like the whole traditional works for lunch. Turkey, celery, walnut and apricot stuffing. Roast spuds. As many different vegetables as I can make, with lots of gravy made from those turkey giblets. Xmas pudding of course, burning with brandy flames. Coffee, Turkish delight, chocolates, multi-coloured cigarettes. Must cut down on crackers. Too expensive. Just a few for the young ones. Adds colour to the table. A.'s old aunts say they feel part of the family again.

Usually about 19 for the day. Sometimes gather not only family but visitors from abroad, or lame ducks lost in town. After lunch the combined effects of food, drink and a warm fire send some to sleep while my helpful kids wash up and I potter around planning supper. Last year we played cards. One year playwright Brian Clark joined us, pushed us into a lovely sing-song. The TV seduces some.

For supper offer a mixture: salmon cutlets, smoked salmon, chopped liver, egg salad, cheeses, peppermint cake, lots of mince pies, fresh fruit. Always amazes me that people can eat after the enormous lunch they put away. But they do! It goes, it goes.

And then we do it all over again next day. Boxing Day dinner. My sister-in-law makes that. Sometimes I envy the lucky ones who go off on winter holidays to the sun. They miss having to give and go to parties, having to give or receive presents. Can't decide whether they're mean or wise.

And this Christmas may be the last one we have in Bishops Road! I've finally persuaded A. to put house on the market. The place where we've spent 24 years bringing up the kids, one way or another. It's too big for us old ones now.

Thursday A.'s back has gone! Pruning roses! Just when I needed him for
5 December Christmas.

Before leaving London, gave lunch to our German agents. Well, they are and they aren't. Krista Jussenhoven and Helmar Fischer ran the drama department of Fischer Verlag. Krista quarrelled with her boss and left. Helmar followed. Now setting up own agency and came to ask A. to join them. Big dilemma. Fischer's are prestigious but A. feels loyalty to people with whom he's had contact over the years rather than to the institution. He'll go with them though some of the plays must stay with agency. They bought rights ages ago. Nothing is simple. Never has been. Sometimes feel I'm the hired chef of a small business concern. Gave them a simple lunch. Prawn salad, and crêpes for dessert.

Prawn Salad

1 cos lettuce, chopped
   (reserve 8 leaves)
6 radishes, sliced
2 tomatoes, sliced
2 sticks celery, chopped
½ cucumber, peeled and sliced
6 stuffed green olives, sliced
1 bunch of watercress, chopped

8 oz / 225 g cooked prawns
4 tablespoons olive oil
2 tablespoons wine vinegar
½ teaspoon dried tarragon
Salt and pepper to taste
1 green pepper, seeds removed,
   cut into rings

Line a large salad bowl with the 8 lettuce leaves. Mix together the salad ingredients and prawns. Pile into bowl.

Combine oil, vinegar, salt, pepper, tarragon. Mix until creamy. Pour over salad. Garnish with pepper rings.

A.'s back is worse. Hobbles around but refuses to see doctor. Can't get him to take an illness seriously. Imagines it'll just go away. *Monday 9 December*

Returned from Wales to find Daniel with eight friends from college. He was singing at a gig. Hauled them along to hear him. They stayed the night. Rooms full of giggling girls and boys settling down on floors all over the house. Next morning kitchen overflowing with youngsters scoffing bacon, eggs, toast and coffee. Shall miss all that when we move. Or will I?

Eran Baniel from Israel joined us for breakfast mêlée. He was passing through, with news about postponed productions of *The Old Ones* and *The Merchant* at Habima Theatre. Slim good news was that Andrei Wajda might direct *The Merchant* later in season! Very slim, I'd say!

Yesterday A.'s agent gave Christmas lunch for clients. Met Henry Kelly and his wife. We're never up early enough to watch his TV AM programme. Says he wants to write, but never has enough time to read. 'And Jesus, you can't write if you don't read!' Our friends the Barries were there, Frank thanking his lucky stars for the American tours of his one-man show *McCready*. Hell for actors depending on this country alone. Hell for any of us depending on this country alone.

Evening attended our first SWET awards, now called the Olivier Awards. Spectacular affair beginning at the Dominion where awards were announced and excerpts shown. Followed by candlelight dinner at the Grosvenor Rooms for about 140, tables of eight each. We were guests of our very generous New York friends, Pat and Ronnie Lee. He runs Group Sales, arranging block bookings to the theatre.

Delicious meal. Melon and avocado salad. Duck suprême, glazed in a passion fruit sauce, with an option for vegetarians of wild mushroom and spinach *vol au vent*. Vegetables and *amandine* potatoes. Iced hazelnut parfait served with raspberry *coulis*. As good as any Jewish wedding. In fact that's what it reminded me of! Considering numbers involved, was very impressed by quality of food and standard of service.

Met the Kinnocks. She told A. she'd been an excited student in Cardiff when he'd lectured about Centre 42. 'You were God,' she told him. 'Those were heady days.' Christ! That aged us. Kinnock and A. got into a brief, heated exchange about letter A. had written him hauling him over the coals for glib remarks he'd made in a John Mortimer interview about the so-called 'angry generation' of playwrights. Kinnock hadn't replied. A. was going to avoid bringing it up. Kinnock did. He shouldn't have. Got himself in a tangle about something he didn't really understand. Turned to his wife and explained: 'Arnold here wrote me a letter giving me a bollocking and I didn't reply and now he's quite rightly giving me another bollocking.' Later saw them both race away upstairs unaccompanied. They'd given up a whole evening in a packed, busy life. Why wasn't anyone in the show-biz world accompanying them to the door?

East German radio man for tea tomorrow. They want to do *Bluey*. Will bake him a cake.

Thursday
12 December

Baked him a chocolate almond cake. Mr Dieter Grollmintz. Tall and too charming. Clicked his heels and kissed my hand. But he ate two portions of the cake!

Bluey was transmitted on Radio 3 last night. Two years after it was written. Didn't stay to listen to it. We'd heard it on an advanced tape. Planned instead to support our good friend Sheila doing Walton's *Façade* at the Queen Elizabeth Hall. Fun, but an impossible piece.

Bluey was European Radio Commission for 1984. Our first play specially written for the medium. Out it went, cold. No party. No word from anyone at the BBC. No sense of occasion. No good-luck message. No thank you. When the plays were done on TV, I'd make dinner for cast and technicians and we'd all sit on the floor watching the box. Perhaps I should've made a spread for the radio play. I grow old.

Out for dinner tonight. Old friends and someone else's cooking. Luverly!

Chocolate Almond Cake with Peppermint Icing

4 oz / 100 g butter
4 oz / 100 g sugar
2 eggs
3 oz / 75 g drinking chocolate
2 oz / 50 g ground almonds

5 oz / 150 g self-raising flour
½ teaspoon vanilla
2 tablespoons hot water
2 tablespoons milk

Grease 8 in / 20 cm cake tin.

Cream butter and sugar. Beat in eggs. Fold in drinking chocolate, ground almonds and self-raising flour. Add vanilla, hot water, milk. Bake at 180°C / 350°F / gas mark 4 for 40 minutes or until firm to touch.

Peppermint icing

2 oz / 50 g milk chocolate polka
  dots
1 oz / 25 g butter

½ teaspoon peppermint essence

Melt chocolate and butter. Remove from heat. Add peppermint. Spread over cake.

Six days to Christmas. A. on his back most of this week with muscular spasms. I'm praying he'll be on his feet soon, unless that's the way he prefers to spend Christmas! *Friday 20 December*

Torn between writing this as a journal of feeding people and as a diary of daily events. Days are full of such interesting details. Good and bad, weird and wonderful, hopeful and depressing: the visit of a cabalist who engaged A. in debate about life after death while he was stretched on his back on lounge floor; Tricycle Theatre want to do *The Kitchen* with mainly black cast – A. wants to suggest that they commission Magda to write a West Indies version of *Roots*; critics on radio ignored *Bluey*; A. started work on a new one-act play for Sheila to accompany *Yardsale* which was also written for her; someone from

Argentina came for tea whose sister wants to do *The Four Seasons* in Buenos Aires; A. has interview with Canadian Broadcasting Corporation direct by telephone . . . But I must press on.

Almost daily visits to supermarket. Stocking up. Lots of people to feed. Made five dozen mince pies ready to pop into oven, and three cakes. One for Magda and L.J., one for Marina my hairdresser – friend of the family now – and one for us. All marzipanned and iced. The puddings were done last month, boiled nine hours so they only need another two.

Am grateful this time of year for my endless pots of stock from past chickens. All stored and waiting in freezer, along with Mum's french beans and the raspberries we picked in July.

And isn't next week going to be hectic! Eleven for dinner on Monday, ten on Tuesday, twenty-one for Christmas lunch on Wednesday. Thank God I'm organised, if nothing else. Plan pheasant for Monday. Bought them in advance so I could joint and clean them. Safely tucked away in freezer which groans with abundance. As I write, the backbones are boiling with carrots and onions. Good stock for gravy. I'll give them raspberries and cream for dessert.

For Tuesday contingent plan something with chicken breasts, also in freezer. I'll take them out on Monday and flatten them ready to roll in pâté and serve with lots of cream sauce, mushrooms and sweetcorn fritters. Think I'll make little cheese soufflés as starter, though that'll mean I'll have to be in kitchen up to last minute. Can't be helped. That's what I fancy. And for afters – two summer puddings bursting to get out of that overworked freezer.

For the big lunch? Never serve a starter at Christmas. Ordered 23 lb turkey today. That should feed 'em all and leave pickings for days after.

People are funny this time of year. They've dieted so carefully in the months leading up to hog-yourself day that they go mad. Suddenly. They'd eat *you*, if you stood still long enough.

Each year declare: next time round I'll spend somewhere with my feet up. Probably never will. Christmas morning too special for my family. Just doesn't feel like Christmas. There's no snow. Need snow to complete picture for me. On the other hand I've been wrapping parcels these past weeks. Neat piles of Christmas gifts scattered around are really all I need to convince me it surely must be Christmas.

Will spend next days delivering them. Plastic bagfuls, each one tagged and named by family: the Saltiels, the Grooms, the Appignanesis . . . And each parcel labelled for the individual: Miles, Flick, Adam, Julie, Della, Ralph, Jane and Jonathan . . .

Fondly imagine I'm well ahead but, come Christmas morning, there's always more to do than I've remembered. Just trying to keep everything hot for twenty-one people between kitchen and dining room is problem enough.

One down, two to go. Being organised allows me to snatch a moment to write. It was a good evening. Our old friend, Anne Cuneo, a Swiss writer and director who's directing *Annie Wobbler* in Zürich, arrived yesterday to spend Christmas with us. She's high, tense, exhausted and in despair with the actress. Not her own choice. I've seen A. in such a state. When an actor is out of control, there's no misery quite like it. Always felt helpless in such a crisis but with Anne it'll be different – I can make a Christmas for her.

Monday's dinner was for Lottie, Chris, their two girls, Zoe and Daisy. Daisy is A.'s god-daughter. Lottie was an actress in *The Kitchen* twenty-six years ago! Chris is a stockbroker. A. keeps threatening to visit his offices. Wants to write a play about money.

Tuesday
24 December

Also invited Jocelyn, Jan-Otto and his two children. Jocelyn was head of public relations for Air Canada in Europe. Met Jan-Otto on a plane. He's a banker, works for Rothschild's in London, and is a baron, which makes her a baroness. Curious how none of us take such titles seriously any longer. *They* don't seem to, either. Invited Nikki whom we don't see enough, that is what happens when married friends split.

Jan-Otto came straight from Heathrow – he'd been visiting the French Rothschild's in Paris 'to brief them on de-nationalisation'. He explained: 'Mitterrand is having to re-privatise a lot of what he's nationalised.' A. tackled him about that over dinner, despite the fact that I sat him at the head of the table with Moore girls on either side. Thought that would please them. First time they'd been allowed to stay awake for a grown-up dinner. Anne retired early. Nikki stayed late.

Broken day. Long talks with Daniel about college; a visit from A.'s nephew, Adam, who got high on a bottle of wine and lingered till we sat down for dinner. He's studying psycho-therapy. Made a great impression on Jocelyn.

Everyone seemed to enjoy meal. Delicious celery soup for starters. Served pheasant with parsnips, green beans and finely sliced carrots. Dessert of lemon soufflé with sweet raspberry cream as contrast. Raspberry cream called for touch of lemon which is often used to bring out other tastes. I put in too much. For *my* palate anyway. Guests enjoyed the contrast. And the children helped with serving and clearing away, which relaxed the atmosphere. Think friends are grateful when their children are included.

What a lot of sensations we go through in a day!

Celery Soup

1 large onion, finely chopped	2 pints / 1.2 litres chicken stock
1 lb / 450 g celery, chopped	¼ pint / 150 ml single cream
2 oz / 50 g butter	1 tablespoon chopped parsley

Using large saucepan, cook onion and celery in butter for 10 minutes. Add stock. Bring to boil. Leave to simmer for 30 minutes. When cool, liquidise together with cream. Reheat. Serve hot with chopped parsley sprinkled on top.

1 pheasant, jointed	1 teaspoon chopped parsley
4 oz / 100 g butter	¼ pint / 150 ml port
4 sticks celery, chopped	Salt and pepper to taste
½ pint / 300 ml chicken stock	1 egg yolk, beaten
2 rashers bacon, diced	½ pint / 300 ml single cream

Using heavy-bottomed casserole, melt butter and brown pheasant pieces all over. Add the celery, then stock, bacon, parsley and port. Season to taste. Cover and simmer for 1 hour. Remove pheasant pieces and vegetables with slotted spoon on to serving dish. Put aside and keep hot. Mix beaten egg yolk with cream. Gradually stir into hot stock. Do not reboil. Pour over pheasant pieces. Serve immediately.

Lemon Soufflé

1 packet lemon jelly	3 large eggs, separated
½ pint / 300 ml water	3 oz / 75 g castor sugar
Juice of 2 large lemons	½ pint / 300 ml double cream
Grated rind of 2 large lemons	

Dissolve jelly in water and lemon juice. Add lemon rind. Leave to cool but not to set. Beat yolks. Add sugar gradually. Stir into lemon jelly mix. Whip egg whites until stiff. Fold in. Whip cream. Fold in.
   Pour into soufflé dish. Leave to set for a few hours.

And that was Christmas.
   Bit like fireworks night – all that collecting and storing and then, *Friday* suddenly, gone. Into the air. And, in between each mouthful, life *27 December* continues with deaths and births and separations. Could fill these pages with so much private pain and strangeness. But it's supposed to be a journal of feeding people, not revealing them.
   After the Monday dinner, had a problem. Always lay my Christmas lunch table the day before, so couldn't sit Tuesday family guests in dining room. Kitchen too small because, as usual, numbers grew. Twelve by the day's end. Had to be a hot buffet served from

kitchen for laps in the lounge. Changed my menu. Instead of rolling chicken breasts in pâté, cooked them with mushrooms and sour cream and fennel, served with saffron rice and green beans. Had cold sliced tongue and salad lying around in case! Dessert was just my old trifle. Fresh raspberries and cream as an alternative. Oh yes, and some mince pies, which always go well with coffee.

Reason for gathering: to entertain the visiting Israeli boy-friends of A.'s cousins' daughters. A close family!

Xmas morning started more slowly than usual. Tried but failed to persuade L.J. and Magda to stay overnight with Natasha. Had to wait for them to arrive. In the past everyone just rolled out of bed and down the stairs. A. made the traditional smoked salmon sandwiches (thanks to Tom Maschler who buys us a whole side every Christmas). Made large pot of PG Tips, lit the fire and we all settled round the tree. Natasha, to my delight, very content to watch everything from my lap.

It's a ritual. We're in dressing gowns. Together with A., I hand the wrapped gifts to each member of the family. (Anne, our old Swiss friend, was not forgotten.) Some let them pile up, others open them as they come. Everyone is armed with pencil and paper to record what came from whom – insisted from childhood they write and thank people. Plastic sacks lie around for the discarded paper. The air fills with groans, sighs, delight and laughter. Soon we're all kissing one another for what's been bought, stretching across the confusion of jumpers, knickers, blue and white china, bottles of wine, jars of dried herbs, packets of coloured stationery, perfume, books, records, scarves, gloves, cassettes, torn gift paper, coloured bows, string, baby toys . . . Guess who had the most presents! Her first Christmas. Sounds of pleasure as her first building toys were unwrapped. She loved my jack-in-the-box. Extra special this year.

Hardly time to clear away before first guests arrived for drinks. Offered glogg. Used a recipe picked up in Sweden. We think our winters are cold but there they need such a drink. Though I didn't cook a turkey for Jackson's Lane Community Centre this year, A. felt he had to go and help carve, leaving me to top up glasses and dart into the kitchen to start things off. I'd started the turkey at 6 a.m.! Protected by tin foil till the last hour. Puddings to steam, potatoes to roast. They're easy. But at the last minute I have to do the beans, sprouts, peas . . . Making sure everyone's served a hot meal will always be an effort for me. Needless to say most people are half way through before I'm sitting down to mine. We pulled crackers, proposed toasts. The old aunts declared they wouldn't miss it for the world, and the turkey carved beautifully.

As usual the children (children?) took over washing up. I laid out table for supper. Friends came. Aunts dozed. Scrabble played. More food eaten.

Boxing Day lunch with Nikki Gavron, dinner with Della and Ralph. The family again. Food again.

Chicken Breasts in Sour Cream and Fennel

6 chicken breasts	4 oz / 100 g mushrooms, chopped
1 head of fennel	
½ pint / 300 ml chicken stock	1 oz / 25 g flour
1 oz / 25 g butter	Salt and pepper to taste
1 medium onion, chopped finely	½ pint / 300 ml sour cream

Cut fennel into thin slices. Poach in chicken stock for 10 minutes. Remove with slotted spoon and set aside. Melt butter and cook onion and mushrooms for 5 minutes. Remove onion and mushrooms with slotted spoon. Slice chicken lengthwise. Cook in butter for 10 minutes. Remove with slotted spoon. Add flour to butter to make roux. Let out with chicken stock. When creamy, add chicken pieces, onions, mushrooms, fennel slices, salt and pepper to taste. Cover and simmer for 15 minutes. Remove from heat. Stir in sour cream.

Serve with saffron rice.

Glogg (Swedish Christmas Drink)

2 bottles claret	4 sticks cinnamon
1 small bottle aquavit	2 tablespoons grated orange rind
½ lb / 225 g sugar	2 oz / 50 g raisins
10 cardamoms, crushed	2 oz / 50 g blanched almonds
10 cloves	

Pour wine into saucepan. Add sugar and spices, orange rind and raisins. Simmer slowly without boiling until sugar is dissolved. Add alcohol. Heat up, then light with match and wait for aquavit to burn down. Add the almonds. Serve very hot, in mugs, on cold winter days.

Stuffing for Turkey of around 20 lb / 9 kg

2 medium onions, chopped
1½ oz / 40 g butter
Small head of celery, finely
  chopped
4 oz / 100 g dried apricots,
  soaked overnight

4 oz / 100 g chopped walnuts
8 oz / 225 g fresh breadcrumbs
2 tablespoons chopped parsley

Cook onions in butter until soft. Add celery, apricots, walnuts and cook for about 5 minutes in order to combine ingredients. When cool, add breadcrumbs and parsley. Stuff the bird!

Mincemeat for Mince Pies

8 oz / 225 g seedless raisins
2 medium apples, chopped
2 oz / 50 g almonds, chopped
6 oz / 175 g candied peel
8 oz / 225 g beef suet
8 oz / 225 g brown sugar
Grated nutmeg

Grated rind of 1 lemon
Juice of 1 lemon
2 tablespoons brandy
2 tablespoons rum
1 teaspoon allspice
½ teaspoon salt

Mix all ingredients and put in closed container until needed.
  Can be used with either shortcrust or almond pastry.

Tuesday
31 December

Just returned from Lewisham. The Barries' 25th wedding anniversary luncheon. More smoked salmon, more champagne! On the way dropped off letter for Pinter which he and A. are co-signing for *The Guardian*, about continued imprisonment of the Turkish Peace Association executive. Our friend, Ali Taygun, the cuddly actor/director who translated *The Merchant* into Turkish, was a member. Will Turkish authorities ever permit play to be performed now?

Brief respite till our New Year's party, called for 10 p.m. New Year's Eve is a depressing time for many people. The idea to have a gathering was a last minute one. Amazed at the number who'd no plans to welcome in the new year. How can you do that? ask I who, incidentally, am hoping to move house in the new year so I don't know what problems *I'm* welcoming in! Barries are making a return visit to join us!

Wanted to see three people before the main rush. Guy Slater whom I've not seen for months. A. met him in Cuba in 1968, actor/son of the British Ambassador, now a TV producer, writer and director. Came with his girl-friend, Julia Scofield, also a writer. And Pamela. Imagine! she'd planned to spend New Year's Eve on her own! In bed! Wasn't having any of that. We've become very close since she designed that brilliant set for *Annie Wobbler*. Offering them leg of lamb with jacket potatoes, some salad. Nothing too elaborate. Might do a zabaglione for dessert. Easy and exotic.

But what to offer our New Year guests? They'll all have eaten themselves stupid by now but – put food in front of people and they'll eat! I'm not one of those cooks who can make rissoles out of leftover turkey. Can't disguise half-eaten dishes to look like something new. Yesterday made a batch of small meatballs. They can pick at those with cocktail sticks. Some hot quiches. Don't often make them. Prepared them with vegetarian ingredients, because one of my dearest guests might be offended by bacon and prawns! Still have some mince pies in the freezer. And Lindsay and Magda bought us six bottles of champagne for Christmas. Yes, we should be OK.

The New Year is in!

Wednesday
1 January 1986

Last night's festivities under way and the lounge soon thick with people all talking to one another. Feel very relieved when that is happening. L.J. positioned radio for Big Ben's chimes. Champagne bottles lined up ready to be popped. On the first stroke we uncorked, poured, raised our glasses, kissed one another, exchanged New Year resolutions – those of us who dared to vow them! Most people were gone by 1 a.m. Della, Ralph, Nichola, her Peter, and Mary (McMurray) lingered. Like Mary very much. She's direct, strong and warm. Hope one day she'll direct something of A.'s. I know *he* wants to work with *her*.

But a crazy night. Natasha stayed up to see in her first new year, riding high in grandma's arms. I ignored those professional mums who believe all babies should be in bed by seven. She stayed up till 1.30 a.m. and it was one hell of a job to get her down. Her mum and dad were out at a party, so we were left not only to clear up after everyone left, but to baby-sit as well. What a night we had. By the time we were ready to go to sleep she was awake again. Would she go down? Not on your life! Neither in her cot nor in our bed. And though it was lovely having a baby between us again we had to stay awake till 6 a.m. Till mum and dad returned.

And then we had to be up in time to join sister, nephews, cousins and second cousins for our annual New Year's Day dim sum lunch in China town! Family again. Food again.

We've just returned. I'm pooped. All done for another year.

Meatballs

1½ lb / 675 g minced beef	1 medium onion, grated
1 oz / 25 g breadcrumbs	1 pint / 600 ml beef stock
2 eggs	Salt and pepper

Mix together all ingredients except stock. Roll into small balls. Drop these into boiling stock. Cook over gentle heat for 45 minutes.

Zabaglione

5 egg yolks	½ pint / 300 ml Marsala wine
4 tablespoons castor sugar	

Whisk three ingredients together well. Transfer to double boiler. Cook on low heat until mixture thickens and coats back of a wooden spoon. Pour into tall glasses. Serve while hot with dainty biscuits.

Thursday
2 January

Or so I thought. Someone said this morning: 'Thank goodness it's all over.' Not for me. Martyn Naylor is back in town. A very English gent who's run an advertising agency in Tokyo these past 18 years but whose real passion from childhood is theatre. Called from Tokyo to say he'd be in London this weekend. My first thought was: I bet he hasn't had his traditional Christmas lunch, I'll make him one! He's coming with the Japanese actor, Takahida, who's just played King Lear in Tokyo.

Think I'll invite our ex-agent, Robin Dalton, and Bill Fairchild. Haven't seen them for ages. Robin's gone into film production. Her first film is due out soon, others being set up. What energy! And at an age when most people think of retiring. Bill still writes film scripts. His oldies are part of our early years. *Morning Departure, Outcast of the Islands, Star.* Love his anecdotes about Noël Coward. The children will join us, of course. Wonder what disaster stories Robin will bring. Fond times we've all had together.

So, just been out buying ingredients for Christmas pudding and mince pies which, alas, have disappeared and need replenishing. Even managed to find a small turkey. Here I go again.

Yesterday hectic. In the morning, a call from an old acquaintance, Thomas Bresdorf, Danish theatre critic. He's in town researching a book on Sylvia Plath. Was bringing presents from Ole and Elsa. Insisted he could come only on that day. Arrived with a friend as the 'second-Christmas' lunch guests were leaving, bringing with him three beautiful cut-glass tumblers. They sat and drank whisky but we had to take Daniel back to college in Farnham and then go on to Pamela's birthday party in Roehampton. No time to be hospitable. *Monday 6 January*

Robin, needless to say, did have a disaster story. She had her first flight on Concorde and managed to communicate her terror of planes to that elegant plane which then proceeded to malfunction. For the first time in Concorde's history all the passengers had to disembark via the chute. Apparently it's happened six times since. A. was never afraid of flying until he took a trip to Paris with her many years ago – to meet Pierre Cardin who wanted to produce a musical of *The Kitchen*, but greedily wanted too large a percentage. So it never happened. My husband! She gripped A.'s hand on take-off and passed on a fear it took him years to overcome.

Pamela cooked something quite delicious: hot chicken livers on a bed of winter salad, followed by duck in orange sauce with new potatoes and *haricots verts*. Orange bavarois for dessert. Now *she's* my kind of woman. Teaches stage design, designs for the big companies (and all the headaches that involves), brings up two girls without help, and still finds time to maintain friendships, entertain and cook wonderful dishes. She's one of those, along with such as Nikki Gavron, Robin Dalton and A.'s sister and cousins, all of whom are as qualified as I am to write a cook book.

Feel a need to see Doris (Lessing). It's been too long. Must try and get her over for a Sunday lunch. Fuss over her. She doesn't like large gatherings. Think I'll do a lamb casserole. Lamb again, I know. But what can I do, I love lamb. Would eat it every day if I could. Selfish cook, really. Only give people what *I* like!

Photo of Bishops Road house in the Anscombe and Ringland advert of Houses for Sale in the *Ham and High*. That's it then, isn't it!

Thursday
9 January

A. reports very amusing evening with Harold Pinter re-working letter to *Guardian* about the Turkish Peace Association. Cuts all over the place. 'I think we should be economical on emotion,' Harold had said. A. is very fond of him. Wants to have the Pinters and Osbornes round for dinner one evening before we leave this house. Says he feels very protective about them. God knows why. *He's* the one needs protecting!

Must also line up a lunch party Sunday 19th before A. flies off to attend his first nights. *The Friends* opens in Modena, the first stage of an Italian tour; *Annie Wobbler* opens in Zürich; and the British Council have invited him to read *Annie* in Paris. We're hoping the Lyons production of *Annie* will end up in the capital. Thank God for foreign productions I say, or we'd really be up the creek. Didn't press to join him this trip, partly because of cost and partly because I want to go when there's sunshine, a good dose of which I badly need. He's been invited to read *Annie* at the Parma Festival in April. I'll accompany him then. They pay for wives.

Friday
10 January

On 19th we have visiting us a brilliant young law student from Harvard, Deborah Holmes. Was going to invite our law friends, Nicho and Percy Browne-Wilkinson, but Deborah took so long to write confirming she was able to come that Sunday (in fact A. had to send another card to ask again) that it was too late to get them. Shall never get used to how casual people are about arrangements while I race around scheming and plotting to make an event as special as possible.

Have invited David Edgar and Eve Brook. David's on his back – does every man suffer with his back? Eve thinks he'll be up by the 19th. Haven't seen her since she lost a brother and two nephews in the Bradford football stadium fire. She's been elected Labour candidate for a Birmingham ward. The other couple are Heather Couper and Nigel Henbest. Astronomers. Never met an astronomer. Heather and A. shared a morning radio programme some months ago, was very taken with her. He enjoys bright energetic women who make him laugh! Nigel's her business associate. They're vegetarians. Thank goodness she's given me good notice. Don't even eat fish! Can't impose vegetarian food on all my guests. Will have to make something special for the two of them. Vegetarian moussaka perhaps, and some gnocchi.

Mary McNaught Davis rang this evening. A neighbour. Moving from her house up the road. Wanted to know would we come for drinks. Help her say goodbye to Highgate. Soon we'll be doing the same, I hope. She says it's brought her to the verge of a nervous breakdown. What will it do to *us*? I'm game for the challenge but A. has difficulty letting go of anything. His study is full of hoarded bits and pieces he can't discard. The contents of his room will slowly drown him if I don't get him out. But his gloomy face, whenever the subject comes up, is intimidating. He makes me fear it'll be the wrong decision.

Drinks with Mary are on the day we have Deborah, the Edgars and the astronomers to lunch. Think I'll be organised enough to go.

Must remember to send a telegram tomorrow to Zeynep in Istanbul. She's getting married.

Daniel rang proudly to announce high marks for his first end-of-term essays. I was chuffed to think he cared about us knowing.

Five for today's lunch. Doris came early. Good! We could natter about family and friends. She's another great cook. Known her all my married life. She came to our wedding 27 years ago. Strong opinions but gentle. No edge, no sarcasm, no bitterness. A disciplined lady who neither offends nor takes offence. When she's working she lets *Sunday 12 January* you know. Because she's relaxed she makes me feel relaxed. We often recall the details of my wedding which she declares was the best she ever attended.

It *was* a good wedding. Didn't know how to cook in those days so we spent A.'s Arts Council Award, which he'd received for his play *Chicken Soup With Barley*, on hiring caterers. There were 250 guests, Irish dancers, a film show, Dick Williams's live jazz band. Held it in the Primrose Jewish Youth Club on the Finchley Road, run by Della and Ralph. Funny incident as my folks arrived from Norfolk through the front door. Della's two kids thundered down the stairs and the table carrying the wedding cake wobbled and pitched the three-tiered thing forward on to the floor. Instant Roman ruins! My parents thought it catastrophic. Shocked when we laughed.

The other guests at the Sunday lunch were D. A. N. Jones, journalist and novelist, and his wife, Lesley, a teacher. He's in the middle of a cycle of seven novels. First one is about sloth. 'I understand that,' said Doris, 'I'm full of sloth.' What *she* meant was that she hadn't been writing for two months. Nothing, that is, except the libretto for an opera which Philip Glass was composing, based on one of her novels. David goes even further back than I do in A.'s life, a student in Balliol, Oxford, when A. was an RAF conscript stationed in nearby Moreton-in-the-Marsh.

Had two shoulders of lamb boned out yesterday so as I could be prepared for this morning. Made an aubergine mould to go with the casserole. Did that yesterday. Also an apple and apricot pie. Lattice-topped it. Always looks pretty. Gave them honeydew melon for starters. Prided myself that, by my standards at least, I'd offered a slimming meal. Though as I think about it, the pastry *was* made with butter and I did offer whipped cream on top! Melted in your mouth however. And guests didn't complain. Don't suppose guests ever can, poor things.

Ended hectically, like a suddenly speeded-up movie. L.J. popped in to record something on video and eat left-overs; Della stopped by to say hello to Doris. A.'s cousins, Norma and Mike, called in to return dresses Norma had borrowed for a wedding. Norma, also a teacher, instantly in conversation with Lesley. Doris faced the comings and goings with grace then, very suddenly and definitely, stood up and apologised that she had to leave.

Had Tanya and Natasha all day yesterday. My lovely gals. A. took Tanya home and then drove to friends Lisa and John to read them his new one-act play *Whatever Happened To Betty Lemon?* They'd retired early as weary, pregnant ladies and their men often do. He read to them in bed. The play's first airing. They laughed and loved it, he reported. Were they being honest? I asked him. He said not even friends can hide real discomfort if it's felt. I'm not so sure.

Lamb Casserole

3 lb / 1.3 kg shoulder of lamb, boned and cut into cubes
1 carrot, sliced
1 large onion, sliced
Juice of 1 lemon
Salt and black pepper to taste
Bay leaf
2 cloves garlic, crushed

2 tablespoons vegetable oil
1 tablespoon flour
4 tablespoons tomato purée
½ teaspoon oregano
4 tablespoons chopped parsley
8 oz / 225 g tin of plum tomatoes
8 oz / 225 g tin of kidney beans

Boil lamb bones in 1 pint / 600 ml water with carrot, onion, lemon juice, bay leaf, salt and pepper. Simmer for 1 hour. Strain. Leave aside.

Using a heavy ovenproof casserole, brown the cubed lamb, with garlic, in oil for about 10 minutes. Stir in flour so that meat is coated. Let out with lamb stock. Add tomato purée, oregano, parsley, tomatoes and kidney beans. Simmer until lamb is tender.

Aubergine Mould

2 large aubergines, thinly sliced
2 tablespoons olive oil
1 large onion, finely chopped
2 cloves garlic, crushed

8 oz / 225 g tin of Italian tomatoes
½ pint / 300 ml plain yoghurt
Salt and pepper to taste

Sprinkle aubergines with salt. Leave for 30 minutes. Rinse and dry with kitchen paper.

Fry aubergines in olive oil, a few minutes each side. Remove with slotted spoon. Leave to drain on kitchen paper. Fry onion and garlic for 10 minutes. Add tomatoes, salt and pepper.

Grease a deep dish. Place alternate layers of aubergine, yoghurt and tomato and onion mix. Bake, covered, at 180°C / 350°F / gas mark

4 for 40 minutes. Cool and turn out. Serve with my recipe for fresh tomato sauce (page 149).

Apricot and Apple Tart

1 lb / 450 g shortcrust pastry (page 13)
2 lb / 900 g cooking apples, peeled, cored and sliced

½ pint / 300 ml pint water
1 lb / 450 g dried apricots
4 oz / 100 g brown sugar
1 teaspoon cinnamon

Grease 10 in / 25 cm pie tin. Line with three-quarters of pastry.

Cook apples in water, together with apricots, sugar and cinnamon. Leave to cool. Fill pastry case with fruit. Use remaining pastry to create lattice top. Bake at 180°C / 350°F / gas mark 4 for 30 minutes.

*Monday
20 January*

Lots of old acquaintances at Mary McNaught Davis's farewell Sunday morning. She *is* in a state. Was surprised we were going off to our own lunch. She'd prepared food but had forgotten to inform us!

Mavis and Geoff Nicholson were there, and Stanley and Judy Price. Stanley and Judy know about moving. They seem to do it once every three years. He wrote a play about it. We're all plumper, greyer, more crinkled and rumpled. Think I prefer seeing friends every day, that way you can't see time passing. 'Youngest' among us was 71-year-old Pat Engardi. She was primary school teacher to most of our children. At 68, began writing novels. She was always a couple of notches higher in spirit than most. With success, she's up in the stars!

My lunch guests turned out to be a splendid mix. With Eve a prospective Labour candidate, David full of the revival of *Nicholas Nickleby* and the new play he'd written for Ann Jellicoe's community down in Lyme Regis, the astronomers excited about Halley's Comet, conversation leapt all over the place. Got lost when they began to talk about infinity. Can't get my imagination to focus on something with no beginning and no end. Heather and Nigel were contemplating chartering a plane for friends to get up close to the comet. A. fantasised about having enough money to buy a large telescope for Wales, where we have glorious night skies.

Heather promised to advise him.Need to sell the house before we have that sort of spare cash.

My attempts at vegetarian food worked. Made three different dishes. Savoury stuffed peppers, gnocchi and moussaka. 'A vegetarian feast!' exclaimed Heather. Made duck in cherry sauce for the carnivorous ones. And of course a choice of two desserts – apple cheese pie and Bakewell tart. An appreciative table.

Savoury Stuffed Peppers

½ large onion, chopped	1 tablespoon tomato purée
2 tablespoons chopped celery	1 tablespoon chopped parsley
1 tablespoon vegetable oil	1 teaspoon cayenne pepper
8 oz / 225 g can pinto beans, mashed	½ teaspoon cumin
	Salt and pepper to taste
7 oz / 200 g tin of corn	6 medium green peppers
3 tomatoes, chopped	2 oz / 50 g Cheddar cheese,
1 teaspoon basil	grated

Fry onion and celery in oil for 5 minutes. Add all other ingredients to pan except green peppers and cheese. Slice top off green peppers. Remove seeds. Fill peppers almost to top with mixture, then finish filling with cheese. Place peppers in upright position in deep dish with 1 in / 2.5 cm of water. Bake at 190°C / 375°F / gas mark 5 for 35 minutes.

Gnocchi

1¼ pints / 750 ml milk	5 oz / 150 g grated Parmesan
8 oz / 225 g semolina	1½ oz / 40 g butter
2 egg yolks, beaten	Pinch of nutmeg

Grease ovenproof dish.

Heat milk. Add semolina slowly, stirring constantly until thick. Remove from heat. Add beaten egg yolks, 4 oz / 100 g grated cheese, butter and nutmeg. Mix well. Rinse out a dish with cold water. Spoon mixture into wet dish. Leave to cool. Roll into egg-sized balls. Place in prepared buttered dish. Dot with butter, sprinkle with remaining Parmesan cheese. Bake at 220°C / 425°F / gas mark 7 for 15 minutes.

Moussaka

1 large aubergine
3 tablespoons vegetable oil
1 red pepper, cut into strips
2 medium courgettes

3 medium potatotes, peeled,
   boiled and thinly sliced
2 oz / 50 g grated Parmesan
   cheese

Slice aubergine and sprinkle with salt. Leave for 30 minutes. Rinse off and dry on paper towel. Fry aubergine slices in oil. Remove from pan with slotted spoon. Cook red pepper and courgettes until soft. Remove from heat. Add the cooked potatoes.

Cheese sauce

1 oz / 25 g butter
2 tablespoons plain flour
1 pint / 600 ml milk
4 oz / 100 g Cheddar cheese

½ teaspoon nutmeg
½ teaspoon ground bay leaf
Black pepper to taste

Melt butter. Add flour to make roux. Let out with milk. Add cheese. When this has melted, add nutmeg, bay leaf and black pepper.

Tomato sauce

1 large onion, chopped
1 tablespoon vegetable oil
4 oz / 100 g chopped
   mushrooms
Large tin tomatoes

1 clove garlic, crushed
2 tablespoons tomato purée
1 teaspoon oregano
Salt and pepper to taste

Cook onions in oil till soft. Add mushrooms and all other ingredients. Cover and simmer for 30 minutes.

Using an ovenproof dish, layer cheese sauce, aubergines, tomato sauce, aubergines and finally vegetable mix. Sprinkle generously with Parmesan cheese. Bake at 180°C / 350°F / gas mark 4 for 30 minutes.

Apple Cheese Pie

½ lb / 225 g shortcrust pastry
6 eating apples, peeled,
   cored and sliced
8 oz / 225 g ricotta cheese

3 oz / 75 g brown sugar
Small carton yoghurt
2 eggs
1 teaspoon vanilla

Grease 10 in / 25 cm pie tin. Line with pastry. Place slices of apple on pastry, in spirals, each slice over-lapping.

Using mixing bowl, blend cheese, sugar, yoghurt, eggs and vanilla. Pour mixture over apples. Bake at 180°C / 350°F / gas mark 4 for 30 minutes.

Bakewell Tart

8 oz / 225 g shortcrust pastry
3 tablespoons strawberry jam
4 oz / 100 g butter, melted
4 tablespoons ground almonds

4 oz / 100 g castor sugar
3 eggs, separated
½ teaspoon almond essence

Grease 10 in / 25 cm flan tin. Line with pastry. Bake blind at 180°C / 350°F / gas mark 4 for 15 minutes.

Spread jam on baked pastry base. Mix together butter, almonds, sugar, 3 egg yolks and almond essence. Whip egg whites until stiff. Fold into mixture. Pour on top of jam and bake at 190°C / 375°F / gas mark 5 for 40 minutes.

Drove A. to Heathrow. He combines first-night trips with readings and lectures, so it's very much a working schedule. Little time for leisure. Twelve days ahead with no entertaining. Gives me an opportunity to diet. If I can succeed in losing a few pounds it'll encourage me to arrange future dinners with fewer calories. So I tell myself. *Tuesday 21 January*

Tonight Cevat Capan, professor of drama, arrives from Istanbul for three weeks. He's got lots of appointments and can look after himself. Think I'll leave him to do his own catering. Always kid myself the house will be quieter when A.'s away but still people come, and the phone still rings, and the mail still needs to be dealt with every day.

Friday   A. rang from Paris. First night of *The Friends* in Modena had been a
31 January   depressing experience. 'They leave out some and misunderstand the
rest.' Perhaps he shouldn't go to those events, they're such hit and
miss occasions.

Reported a good meeting in Paris with Mort Shuman. Sounds like
my kind of New York Jewish boy. At 16, he'd begun to write hit songs,
among them 'A Teenager In Love' for Dion and the Belmonts. Made a
fortune. Decided not to sit on his laurels. Moved to Paris. Found
himself living in a flat once occupied by a man he'd never heard of
called Jacques Brel. Went on to discover Brel's music and write a
musical called *Jacques Brel Is Alive And Well And Living In Paris*.
Ran seven years off-Broadway and performed around the world.
Shuman remained in Paris. Became a French singing star.

A. had been put in touch with him as possible lyric writer for
musical of *The Kitchen*. They'd got on famously. A. was ringing to say
he and his wife were coming to Sunday lunch on 16th February.
Asked me to invite Michael Nyman, the proposed composer, with his
wife. A slight tension hovers over the confrontation. Mort had been
told by his agent he was being approached to do the music as well. He
comes to the meeting with a degree of half-heartedness. Whatever is
about to happen, I approach with dread and foreboding. That's
awful! What has life done to me? Once upon a time I suspected
nothing and no one.

Coincidentally that day I'd invited David and Paula Swift, Maggie
and Michael Holroyd. That's how my lunch parties grow. But if
Shuman and Nyman want a working session with A., they'll have to
arrive an hour or so before hand. 'Shuman and Nyman'. I turn the
names around on my tongue. Do they sound like a team which will
one day become legendary like Rodgers and Hart, Lerner and Loewe?

Wednesday   Tanya and I met A. at the airport. Henryk had been in town and was
5 February   catching a plane back to Copenhagen around the same time. He was
with us to greet the weary traveller. Lingered over coffee and
exchanged news. Henryk had been having some unpleasant problems at the Royal Theatre as a result of having to cut down on staff. A.
full of horrendous stories about *The Friends* in Italy and *Annie* in
Zürich. But he'd given a successful reading of *Betty Lemon* in Milan,
and there'd been a full house for his reading in Paris. Swings and
roundabouts.

Estate agent rang to make four appointments for people to visit house on Saturday. Some just come in the hope of getting a look at the old man. Makes me mad. 'I suppose,' they say, 'one day there'll be a blue plaque up on the wall.' I feel like saying: 'You interested in the house or sightseeing?' One of them coming is a Mr Farhi. Why is that name familiar?

Discovered why Farhi is a familiar name. Cevat announced that an *Thursday* old school friend with whom he had grown up in Istanbul, Jewish, *6 February* was coming to collect him this morning. His name was Moris Farhi! Invited him to look over house. Preferred to wait till Saturday and come with his wife, a psycho-therapist. But he did peek into the two ground-floor rooms and was at once hooked.

Highgate covered by snow. Garden a wonderland. Cevat leaves today. A.'s agent doesn't like *Betty Lemon*. Sheila doesn't know if she can do the play this year. *Merry Wives* may go to Broadway. She'll decide by June. Who'd be married to a playwright!

Israeli editor coming to see A. tomorrow. Shall I bake a special cake or use up some of the left-over Christmas cake?

Used up left-over Christmas cake. *Sunday*

Three couples came to view on Saturday. The Farhis; an ex- *9 February* diplomat and his stern upper-class wife, the kind who looks slightly disgruntled that her husband was never good enough to become an ambassador; and one couple the man of whom asked: 'Why are there so many photographs of Arnold Wesker in the loo?'

The Farhis confirmed their interest in the house. Are we really going to sell it? It became even more of a possibility when we ourselves viewed a house the other side of Muswell Hill. Both fell for it at once. Our one dread was that moving would involve us living in smaller rooms. This house, though divided into two flats which we'd have to return to one home, contains huge rooms and one that's only a little shorter than our 30 foot lounge. Moving would not be such a rude shock. If we do move, it'll be just when we've established a wisteria in front of the house. Been trying to do so for years.

Today was lunch for mothers, mothers-to-be, children and babies. Lisa and Bernie came with Lindal, our new and fourth godchild. Pregnant Lisa, two and a half weeks to go, came with John and Joshua. L.J. and Magda turned up with Natasha who now walks all the time. Tanya was weekending with us. Poor Lindal was suffering from colic and did quite a bit of crying. Both A. and I tried to soothe her but failed. Magda took over and succeeded. Lisa's tense about it. Knows she communicates anxiety to the child. Very patient though. What a long way away all that seems.

Made them all a good lunch of artichoke soufflé, roast pork and raspberry meringue pie. Well, the roast pork was new! Have to repeat myself sometimes!

Margaret Semil phoned. She's here from Warsaw shepherding a group of dramaturges and directors from the Polish Theatre. Came for tea. Didn't want to eat any left-overs, she's on a diet. Just nibbled cheese and biscuits and talked about their programme and how things were in Poland – 25° below zero for the last four days.

'It's spring here,' she exclaimed. Brought more gorgeous stamps, and news that her literary magazine *Dialog* is going to print A.'s speech to the conference of International Theatre Critics in Rome. She hasn't yet started translating *Annie Wobbler* which she planned for *Dialog*. Promised to do so soon. Theatre in Poland not easy these days. *Dialog* had published *Love Letters On Blue Paper*, translated by Karol, her husband, and *Caritas*, but there was no hope of productions. Some years ago *The Kitchen* had run for three years in Warsaw and other Polish cities. We'd all been able to have a skiing holiday in Zakopane on the royalties. Not that any of us could ski!

Invited her to bring her Poles to tea one day if they were free.

Italian agent rang. Reviews for *The Friends* in Italy are excellent. Anne rang from Zürich. Seems we've got good reviews there, too. A. bewildered. Never look a gift horse . . .

Roast Leg of Pork

5 lb / 2.2 kg leg of pork	Generous amount of black
½ pint / 300 ml water	pepper
2 tablespoons peanut oil	1 teaspoon ground bay leaf
1 tablespoon mustard	1 teaspoon ground ginger

Lay pork in roasting tin with water. Combine oil, mustard, black pepper, ground bay leaf and ground ginger. Rub mixture into skin of pork. Roast at 190°C / 375°F / gas mark 5 for 2 hours basting constantly. Make sure skin turns to crackling. Serve with apple and cranberry sauce.

Apple and Cranberry Sauce

2 large apples	2 tablespoons breadcrumbs
1 medium onion	½ teaspoon powdered mustard
¼ pint / 150 ml chicken stock	1 dessertspoon vinegar
1 tablespoon brown sugar	¼ lb / 100 g cranberries

Peel and slice apples thinly. Slice onion. Simmer in stock and sugar until soft. Stir in breadcrumbs, mustard, vinegar and cranberries. Cover and simmer for 15 minutes. Serve hot.

Have decided what to do for my 50th. Celebrate it over a weekend in the Welsh cottage with friends. Will select six couples, pay their hotel for the night, get someone locally to do the cooking. Want it to be a very relaxed time – log fires, friends, family, another cook's food! Won't be able to get off entirely scot-free. Have to cook Sunday lunch. Will enjoy that, though. Friends knowing each other is half the battle.

Monday
10 February

Last summer A. finished first draft of new play. At last minute decided to enter it for Mobil/Royal Exchange Theatre competition. Entries submitted under a pseudonym. Judges included Joan Plowright who'd created Beatie Bryant in *Roots* 28 years ago. Would she recognise the voice, we wondered? Yesterday heard that though it won no prize, it had been 'spotted'. What did that mean? Had they sensed a professional at work and not been able to resist peeking? Unethical. Should have returned all manuscripts unopened. They offered a rehearsed public reading. We declined. It was a first draft.

Should A. be distressed by the offer? *I* don't think he should have entered competition in first place. But things like that don't upset him as they do me. Despite setbacks, he has a quiet confidence about all he writes. Suspect, even though it's painful, he enjoys being out of step.

Wednesday
12 February

Still haven't decided what I'm cooking for the Shuman/Nyman Sunday lunch. Got two pigeons in the freezer. Always wanted to try out a pigeon pie recipe I discovered. Not everyone likes pigeon. Will have to make additional dishes to give people choice. But what?

Estate agents rang to say another couple want to view house next Saturday. They have to keep coming in case Farhi deal falls through. His surveyor comes next week. What if he finds structural damage, requiring large sums to put right? But we're also having to spend large sums before moving into our new house. Everyone has to. Get so nervous. Just never expect anything to go right. Meanwhile I've asked for estimates from removal people.

Friday
14 February

Natasha's first-year party today. Magda has invited all her friends who've become mothers this year. 'Tash will be the oldest. It'll be a noisy affair. But that little girl loves company. Has no fears. Ordered her a birthday cake in the shape of No. 1. Will make something myself, of course – a couple of large quiches and some trifles for the children. Next year will be another ball game when she's conscious of what a party is.

Saw pheasants in the butchers. Couldn't resist buying them for the freezer. Do for Sunday lunch on my birthday weekend.

Can't stop thinking about the new house. Plan to make it as inviting as this one has been for last 23 years.

Saturday
15 February

Decided on fresh fish. Hake. And as I've got a collection of nice Jewish boys, I'll give them some of their mother's chopped liver. Also found this recipe for chocolate hazelnut cake.

Another couple came to view the house today. Fell in love with it and offered us more than the asking price. Told them we'd promised the first purchaser that we wouldn't let him be gazumped but, that if his surveyor talked him out of the house next Friday, it'd be back on the market.

Monday
17 February

Shuman and Nyman appeared to get on. Discovered a mutual love of rock and roll! Mort's taken a tape of Nyman's music. Everything

Added a pigeon pie to the meal, but fried hake was a success. Gave them a choice of a couple of my favourite starters – artichoke soup and chopped liver. Served *lyonnaise* potatoes, sweet and sour cabbage, cucumber and watercress in yoghurt, endive salad with lots of garlic. Table bubbled with conversation. About Paula's TV series *Albion Market* – thank God A.'s not involved writing soap opera; about David's new career as a TV writer and cook – with Paula in Manchester all week he has to cook for himself! He's loving it. About Mort's life in Paris as a pop star. About Maggie's and Michael's forthcoming lecture-tour in Iceland. Told them how confusing we'd found the country with daylight for most of the night. A table full of some of my favourite people. And what would I do without my loving daughter who always manages to get everything washed up so discreetly?

Farhi family came again to look over the house. Still seem very excited. Hope they don't use surveyor's report to beat down price. That would be foolish. We made it so plain we weren't haggling. They stayed for coffee and left-overs. Tasted the atmosphere they might inherit. Cousins Belle and Alan dropped by. Must say I sometimes enjoy the endless stream.

A. rushed back into town to National Theatre to take part in a day-long roll-call organised by Tom Stoppard on behalf of Soviet Jews in prison. Every minute a famous personality stepped up to a microphone to read out from a list. Drama students threw a red rose on the ground for each name read out by Michael Frayn, Margaret Drabble, Harold Pinter, Neil Kinnock, Richard Hoggart . . .

Pigeon Pie

12 oz / 350 g shortcrust pastry	2 hard boiled eggs
2 pigeons, jointed	4 oz / 100 g mushrooms
6 oz / 175 g minced pork	Salt and pepper to taste
4 oz / 100 g minced veal	1 oz / 25 g butter
½ pint / 300 ml red wine	1 dessertspoon flour
Oil for frying	4 dessertspoons chicken stock

Soak minced pork and veal in ¼ pint / 150 ml of red wine for 1 hour. Line a deep pie dish with half the pastry. Spread half the minced meat mix on the bottom. Fry pigeon joints lightly in oil. Place on top of minced meat, together with quartered eggs. Fry mushrooms. Lay over eggs. Spread on remaining minced meat. Season to taste.

Make a sauce by melting the butter, and stirring in flour to make roux. Let out with stock and remaining wine. Allow to thicken slightly. Pour over pie contents. Cover with remaining pastry. Make a large incision in top to allow steam to escape. Cook at 190°C / 375°F / gas mark 5 for 40 minutes.

Chocolate Hazelnut Cake

4 oz / 100 g butter	4 eggs separated
4 oz / 100 g castor sugar	1 tablespoon instant coffee
4 oz / 100 g drinking chocolate	1 tablespoon rum
4 oz / 100 g ground hazelnuts	

Grease three 8 in / 20 cm sponge tins.

Beat butter and sugar together well. Add drinking chocolate, hazelnuts and egg yolks. Combine coffee with rum. Add to butter mix. Whip egg whites until stiff. Fold in. Pour into three sponge tins. Bake at 140°C / 275°F / gas mark 1 for 1½ hours. When cool, carefully remove from tins and lay on rack.

Cream for filling

1 pint / 600 ml double cream	½ teaspoon vanilla
1 dessertspoon sugar	9 oz / 250 g toasted almonds

Whip cream, sugar and vanilla. Fold in almonds. Spread between layers and over top of the cake.

Thursday
20 February

Am dreading surveyor coming tomorrow, crawling all over the house I've cared for 23 years. But today the world feels a wonderful place because Ted Thorpe's taking me to the ballet. Bumped into him last year at Covent Garden and expressed my love of ballet. He made a new year resolution to take me some time in 1986. Love the atmosphere and enthusiasm of the place. Always regret not getting there more often. Gillian and A. will join us at Joe Allen's afterwards – another of my favourite places.

Strange day yesterday. In the morning A. was part of a P.E.N. demonstration outside Turkish Embassy. They handed a letter to the visiting Turkish Prime Minister. In the evening we were at Queen Elizabeth Hall to see a one-woman show by Turkish actress, Yildiz Kanter, followed by dinner at The Savoy. Who was the guest of honour? The Turkish Prime Minister!

Odd how in these last years we've become involved with the Turks. It's what happens when A. does a lecture tour. Another country enters our horizon. Shall never forget very funny dinner some eighteen months ago, which I gave for the Ambassador and his wife. A. wanted to discuss the plight of their political prisoners. Invited Maggie and Michael Holroyd who'd also lectured in Turkey. Maggie's father had been judge. Thought she'd have more authority than us. At the same time, we had staying in the house a French friend of Armenian descent who had little love for the Turks. Of course we dared not reveal to him who our guests were to be. The Ambassador was accompanied by two armed body-guards – fed them too! So, there was the Turkish Ambassador and his wife in the dining room arguing with Maggie against the system of juries – 'What can common people know about justice?'; in the kitchen were his bodyguards being harangued by Tanya, who never misses a chance to engage the police in argument, while a member of a nationality they were supposed to be on the alert against sat upstairs watching TV! Would've made a bizarre episode in a movie.

Surveyor crawled around all day Friday and half of Saturday. Did not like that one little bit. Hope he gets his report out soon. Terrified we'll lose not only the house we want, but the people who were prepared to pay more for ours. I'm already living there. Have collected brochures on fitted kitchens. Planned which room will be for who and what. Removal people say it'll take them five days to move us! Getting quite excited.

Sunday
23 February

Over dinner at Joe Allen's, Ted confessed to being a chocoholic. Baked him a chocolate peppermint cake and ran it round. He was chuffed.

Farhi just had long session with A. He's haggling. Dropped his offer by £15,000. Presented surveyor's report full of this and that wrong. We reminded him that if this and that weren't wrong the price would

Friday
28 February

be higher. Nothing fundamentally unsound about this house. It's solid. Built by a builder for himself in the 1890s. We could live out the rest of our lives here and nothing much would need to be done. Of course if I had a lot of money I'd renew things and make changes. That's different. A. is angry. We made it clear we were not hagglers. We hadn't haggled with the vendors of the house we wanted. We'd not allowed Farhi to be gazumped. Now we'll lose the house we've bid for. I know it.

Monday
3 March

Realise I've not entertained for over a fortnight. And only one lunch party in nine days' time. Can't think about cooking with house problem hanging over me. Prefer accepting invitations out.

Not that the comings and goings have ceased. But this week A. is on reading tour of the north west and I'm determined to diet.

Thursday
13 March

Last entry. Good news and bad news. Bad news first. We've refused Farhi's offer; the other purchaser has purchased another house; and we've lost the house we'd set our hearts on. Told the estate agent that because people seem to want to haggle, he should raise our price by £15,000. Already had an offer £5,000 above our original asking price. Shall never understand the deviousness of people.

Good news is that our friend and translator Ali Taygun and his colleagues have been released from Turkish prison.

Yesterday's lunch was for old friend, Roger Frith, a poet, and Richard de Marco. Richard runs his own art gallery and performing space in Edinburgh. A live wire. A romantic. An enthusiast. Found everything I cooked 'amazing'. It was only fried whiting fillets in prawn sauce, some potato latkas, courgettes and cauliflower and lemon semolina cake. He's just leased a new space below Edinburgh Castle and wants to see a production there of *The Merchant*. Too late for this year's festival. Could be next year. Feels A.'s work is not done enough in this country. He was a tonic. Sat in the lounge with wide eyes. 'There's so much energy coming off this room,' he said. Always look at A. when people say things like that. Perhaps we'll never move.

4 oz / 100 g prawns	2 tablespoons single cream
1 teaspoon wine vinegar	½ teaspoon cayenne pepper
1 teaspoon lemon juice	2 oz / 50 g butter
2 egg yolks	

Stir vinegar, lemon juice, yolks and cream together in a double boiler over boiling water. Add cayenne pepper. Keep stirring to avoid curdling. Gradually add 1 oz / 50 g butter.

Toss prawns in remaining butter for 5 minutes. (It should be possible to alternately stir the sauce and shake the frying pan.) As soon as sauce begins to thicken, remove pot from hot water to prevent further cooking. Add prawns. Serve alongside fried fish.

Lemon Semolina Cake

3 eggs, separated	Juice of 1 lemon
4 oz / 100 g castor sugar	2 oz / 50 g semolina
Grated rind 1 lemon	½ oz / 14 g ground almonds

Grease 8 in / 20 cm loose-bottomed tin.

Beat egg yolks, sugar, rind and juice together very thoroughly. Add semolina and almonds. Beat egg whites until stiff. Fold into mixture. Bake at 180°C / 350°F / gas mark 4 for 40 minutes.

Index of recipes